Truly Great
Jewish Women
THEN & NOW

ISRAEL BOOKSHOP
Publications

Truly Great Jewish Women
THEN & NOW

RABBI Y. Y. RUBINSTEIN

Copyright © 2021 by Israel Bookshop Publications

ISBN 978-1-60091-846-9

Book design by: Rivkah Lewis

Published by:
Israel Bookshop Publications
501 Prospect Street
Lakewood, NJ 08701

Tel: (732) 901-3009
Fax: (732) 901-4012
www.israelbookshoppublications.com
info@israelbookshoppublications.com

Printed in the United States of America

Distributed in Israel by:
Tfutza Publications
P.O.B. 50036
Beitar Illit 90500
972-2-650-9400

Distributed in Australia by:
Gold's Book and Gift Company
3-13 William Street
Balaclava 3183
613-9527-8775

Distributed in Europe by:
Lehmanns
Unit E Viking Industrial Park
Rolling Mill Road,
Jarrow, Tyne & Wear NE32 3DP
44-191-430-0333

Distributed in South Africa by:
Kollel Bookshop
Northfield Centre
17 Northfield Avenue
Glenhazel 2192
27-11-440-6679

To a special woman

ZISEL CHANA BAS SHLOMO DOV LANTSMAN ע"ה

whose selflessness and devotion
to others was her life.

She was the most giving person,
especially to her children.

May her *neshamah* continue to have an *aliyah*,
and may her children and grandchildren
be a constant source of *nachas*.

Rabbi and Rebbetzin Pinchas Weinberger

Mr. and Mrs. Pinny Ackerman

Mr. and Mrs. Moshe Reisman

Meir Shuvalsky

Mr. and Mrs. Yehuda Zachter

In honor of

PHYLLIS ZACHTER עמו"ש

who is the true embodiment of an *eishes chayil*.

Her constant love and support of her
husband and children know no bounds.

She is a true paragon of *chessed*, someone
who is always devoted to helping the *klal*.

With love and admiration,

Your husband and children

In loving memory of my father

SAMUEL WISEMAN
שלמה זלמן ב"ר אלחנן

who instilled in me a yearning for a relationship
with Hakadosh Baruch Hu, and the desire to
continue to learn, to teach by example, and to
aspire to be among the great Jewish women.

Leah Solomon

לזכר נשמת
חנה ברכה בת ר׳ חיים שלמה הכהן

We are honored to sponsor this book
exploring women in Tanach and saluting
Jewish women everywhere who are
focused on accomplishing much good.

May Jewish women always perceive
challenges as opportunities for personal
and societal growth. May they learn,
with the help of this book, the ways of
the *Imahot*, and may it serve to guide them.

The Meyers of Westwood, L.A.

לעלוי נשמת

האשה המעלה והטהורה

שרה בת יבלחט״א אברהם נ״י

הוצאת זו של הספר

Truly Great Jewish Women…Then and Now

מוקדשת לעלוי נשמות הני יקירי זקנינו וזקנותינו

שלמה בן ישראל ז"ל
שרה בת אברהם ז"ל

יונה יוסף בן משה ז"ל
פסיע בת בנציון ז"ל

יחיאל בן אהרן ז"ל
חיה רבקה בת קלמן ז"ל

יחיאל מיכל בן חיים מאיר הלוי ז"ל
רייזל בת זאב ז"ל

תהי נשמתם צרורות בצרור החיים ויעמדו לקץ הימין

הונצח על ידי צאצאיהם שיחיו

לזכר נשמת

רפאל משה ליב בן הרב יהודה

איש חסד

In loving memory
of our parents

ASHER BLOCKMAN
JOYCE RUBIN BLOCKMAN

MEMPHIS, TENNESSEE

לע"נ

אשר בן משה דוד ז"ל • נחמה בת שלום יצחק ע"ה

and

JACK MILTON GAVANT
JANICE ARLENE GAVANT

ATLANTA, GEORGIA

לע"נ

יעקב מאיר בן משה לייב ז"ל • שיינה בת אבא ע"ה

May the insights acquired from studying this
book be a merit for their souls.

ת.נ.צ.ב.ה.

Dedicated by their children

Moshe and Ann Gavant

Baltimore, Maryland

משה לייב וחיה עלקה גוונט

In loving memory of

DORA ROBERTS ע"ה

who had a beautiful and unshakable *emunah peshutah*.

DEAN: Rabbi B Dunner שליט"א
PRINCIPAL: Mrs R. Weiss

198 Lordship Road
London N16 5ES
020 8800 4719

מיסודו של הרה"ג מוהרר"ד יוסף צבי הלוי דינר זצ"ל
Founder Principal: Rabbi J Dunner זצ"ל

ימי הרחמים והסליחות תש"פ לפ"ק

My very close and revered friend, Rabbi Yehudah Yonah Rubinstein שליט"א has delighted me yet again with a manuscript of the latest addition to his great literary masterpieces, entitled Truly Great... Jewish Women Then... Jewish Women Now.

This compendium of Jewish literature spans the millennia, traverses continents, crosses geographical boundaries and political borders with a singular focus on *she'osani kirzono*. The virtues and values of the quintessential *eishes chayil* are portrayed within the powerful, legendary spotlight created by a master orator and acclaimed author in a language and style bound to resonate with today's generation.

The unique character of this *magnum opus* includes novel insights into some of the well-known personalities of *T'nach*, culled from classic and authoritative sources, and subsequently blended into the everyday lives of contemporary heroines, whether of famous or discreet stature. A clarion call highlighting one's ability and obligation to achieve greatness in our times.

Since our first association as *chavrusos* in Liverpool Kollel some four decades back, Rabbi Rubinstein has been on a non-stop trajectory of *kiruv* and *harbotzas haTorah* across the globe, rubbing shoulders with *Gedolei Yisroel*, famous personalities, students of all stripes and just about everyone else in between! Vignettes of his colourful life are reflected in his inimitable style on the pages as they unfold. This is a book to be read and re-read as an ever increasing powerful source of inspiration.

May Rabbi Rubinstein continue to delight his audiences world over in their upward journeys towards spiritual success.

With my very best wishes and Torah greetings
Rabbi Binyomin Dunner

ישיבת
בית יוסף
גייטסהעד

Gateshead Talmudical College

Rosh Hayeshiva
Rabbi A. Gurwicz

88 Windermere Street, Gateshead, Tyne & Wear NE8 1UB.
Telephone: (0191) 477 2616 Fax: (0191) 490 0480

ב״ה [illegible]

<u>מכתב ברכה</u>

הנה הובא לפני [illegible] מתוך הספר של הגה״צ ר׳ יהודה זאב סגל זצוק״ל, אשר [illegible] במאמרים של גדול ישראל, [illegible] [illegible] [illegible] [illegible]

[illegible] ר׳ יהודה זאב [illegible]

[illegible]

[illegible]

בעזה"י

מכתב ברכה

הובאו לפני עלים לבחינה מספרו החדש של הרב ר' יהודה יונה רובינשטיין
שליט"א, אשר בו הוא מתאר האמהות של כלל ישראל, והאמהות הנשים
צדקניות שהוא זכה להכיר, שבהן, כל אחת מהן, מתקיים האימרא "יש
אם למסורה" כלשונו הצח של בעל העקידת יצחק ז"ל, נשים שקדשו
השם בחייהם ושיכולות לשמש לדוגמא של אם בישראל, והרב ר' יהודה
יונה שליט"א כבר נתמחה גברא בספריו וכתביו הקודמים כאומן במלאכת
הכתיבה, שבעטו המבורך הוא מושך לבבות הקוראים וגם משפיע עליהם
השפעה טובה ומועילה, והמעט שהספקתי לראות מספרו החדש הוא ממשיך
בדרכו המוצלח גם בספר זה, והנני לברכו שיזכה לברך על המוגמר בקרוב
ושספרו החדש ינוב בהצלחה המקווה.

אברהם באאמו"ר הגה"צ מוהר"ר ר' אריה זאב זצוקללה"ה גורביץ

נ.ב. הנני להעיר במש"כ בהקדמת הספר, שלשון חז"ל (עירובין י"ג ע"ב) הוא
שנוח לו לאדם שלא נברא משנברא, ולא טוב לו לאדם, שבודאי כל מה דעביד
רחמנא לטב עביד, ורק האדם במבטו המצומצם היה נוח לו שלא נברא, ואנו
מלומדים לתאר העולם, בנוסח הקדיש, בעלמא די ברא כרעותיה, שהעולם
מתאים לרצון ה' והוא שיהיה פרוזדור לטרקלין של עולם הבא, וכזה הוא הכי
טוב שאפשר, אבל האדם ברצונו למצוא הטרקלין כבר בעולם זה מוצא מקום
להתרעם, וכאותו לשון שאנו מתארים העולם האשה מתארת עצמה שעשני
כרצונו.

Rabbi Michel Twerski

26 Tishrei 5781

My dear friend, Rabbi Y.Y. Rubinstein שליט"א, is a מעין המתגבר, an ever-flowing wellspring of refreshing, thirst quenching water. His sparkling fountain of wisdom is constant in its promise to inspire and inform, to counsel and instruct. Consistent with all of the Rabbi's previous publications, Truly Great Jewish Women Then and Now is yet another precious jewel in Rabbi Rubinstein's literary crown. A hearty Mazel Tov on this wonderful contribution to the scholarship of Klal Yisroel.

With warmest ברכות for הצלחה in this and all endeavors, I am
Most respectfully,

Rabbi Michel Twerski

In the world of Torah, nothing captures the imagination more than Chidush – a novel and imaginative idea.

Rabbi Y.Y. Rubinstein, both in his spoken and written word, is a master of both crafts, combining an original dimension to timeless Torah values.

In this, his latest book, Rabbi Rubinstein has connected qualities of greatness revealed in the lives of great women in Tanach, to reflections of these qualities found in contemporary heroines that he has known.

In doing so, he has achieved a dual purpose. Firstly, with sagacity and scholarship, Rabbi Rubinstein has uncovered nuances of nobility and selflessness in familiar figures from the Torah. That in itself is praiseworthy, enhancing as it does our appreciation of our illustrious forebears. Secondly, by identifying those great qualities, and revealing comparisons on ladies of our time, he has demonstrated how blessed is our nation to have personalities who, by themselves being inspired, in turn inspire us.

This book is at once informative, readable, inspiring and challenging. For, if these ladies who are our contemporaries, have achieved such greatness, what about us?

Rabbi Rubinstein is himself an example of a great man, ever striving for loftier heights, and Klal Yisroel is blessed to be able to enjoy the fruits both of his pen and his spoken word.

May Hashem Yisborach bless him and his family with Hatzlochoch and good health, to continue inspiring Jewish hearts for many happy years to come till 120 years - אמן.

Rabbi Avrohom Katz – Principal Beis Chaya Rochel Seminary, Gateshead, UK.

1 Shipcote Lane, Gateshead NE8 4JA | T: 44 (0) 191 4776450 | F: 44 (0) 191 4783522 | E: office@gjag.co.uk
Principal: Rabbi Katz
Registered Charity No. 1101438

Rabbi Y.Y. Rubinstein has done it again.

As in his previous books, he tackles the issues that confront contemporary seekers, with his rare mixture of readable, enjoyable "conversation" and erudite authenticity.

This time, his subject, great women, takes you both to the women of the Torah, and to women who live the Torah, assimilate it, and make it not only what they know, but who they are.

Rabbi Rubinstein has enabled you to hear the Torah giants. As in his previous books, his unusual mastery of the Alshich opens new vistas for any reader, even those with many years of study behind them.

He has also enabled you to "meet" women who you may learn a great deal from—let them change your life!

Tziporah (Heller) Gottlieb

EDUCATION FOR JEWISH WOMEN
ESTD · 1970
NEVE
נוה ירושלים

Neve Yerushalayim Seminar L'Banot (R"A)
P.O.B. 43016, 1 Beit Yitzchak Street
Har Nof, Jerusalem, Israel
(02) 654-4555 | neve@nevey.org

Friends of Neve College for Women Inc.
111 John Street - Suite 1720
New York, NY 10038
(212) 422-1110 | neveny@nevey.org

Rabbi Y.Y. Rubinstein has asked me to attach some words of *brachah* to his latest *sefer.*

I do so with all the joy of one who delights in the accomplishments of a true friend.

He has succeeded in combining fascinating Torah insights into the lives of the "mothers" of our entire people, with accounts of contemporary *nashim tzidkaniyos* who inspired by their examples and went on themselves to achieve Torah distinction.

Rabbi Rubinstein utilizes a remarkably wide range of Torah sources, and succeeds in blending them together to produce a work which is both erudite and eminently readable.

My *brachah* to him is that *Truly Great Jewish Women… Then and Now* should find its rightful place on the bookshelves of Jewish women across the Torah world, and thus be a *zechus* for him and his entire family.

Dovid Refson

USA Registered Non-Profit 501(c)3 organization #13-3163148
Israel: No. 58-001-526-1 :עמותה רשומה

Contents

Acknowledgments

AFTER I PUBLISHED my last book, *Building Tomorrow*, which is on the subject of *sinas chinam* and how to end it, I had an idea for another book. I started to write *Truly Great Jewish Women—Then and Now*, but I only managed four chapters and then, inexplicably, my enthusiasm vanished. I kept reminding myself that the idea for the book (which obviously came from the Source of all ideas, Hashem Himself) was really exciting, but still it remained stuck at four chapters.

Then the corona virus struck, and my traveling around the world to speak came to a halt. My new destination was my home, day after day, and suddenly this book came to life! Chapter after chapter found itself being written. One of my sons told me he had seen in a *sefer* that every book has a time to be written, and it simply cannot be rushed. And so it was with this book.

I am very blessed to have found the perfect team to bring my projects to fruition. Israel Bookshop Publications' founder, Reb Moshe Kaufman, and his head staff members, Mrs. Liron Delmar and Mrs. Malkie Gendelman, are always a delight to work with. I am lucky to have them. Additionally, I am once more deeply indebted to my long-time editor, Mrs. Suri Brand. Her work is always superb.

I would also like to acknowledge my *talmidos* at Elyon Seminary in Brooklyn. They have been a pleasure to teach and were the first to be exposed to some of the early ideas that grew into this book.

I am especially grateful to the members of my weekly women's *vaad* who heard all of the Torah in this book over the course of a year, and helped me refine and polish it. I cannot thank you all enough. You have been a joy to teach, and your questions and input were invaluable.

To my children and grandchildren, who always inspire me and give me such *nachas*: I hope *you* get *nachas* from this latest book.

To the *gedolim*, *chashuve rabbanim*, and *rebbetzin* who added their letters of support to this work: I am humbled and very grateful.

To my dear wife Elisa, who is my greatest support, and who helps me with the early edits of my books, solves my frustrations, and encourages my ideas: thank you.

Lastly, I return to acknowledge and give thanks to the One about Whom we say in the *Amidah* three times every day, "*Atah chonein l'adam da'as*—You give a person knowledge and ideas," Hashem Yisbarach.

Introduction

WHEN THE TORAH discusses the birth of a girl, it makes a very clear distinction to the birth of a boy. When a boy is born, the mother becomes *tamei*, spiritually impure, for a period of seven days. She then has to count another thirty-three days before she can bring a *korban* to the Beis Hamikdash and her *tamei* status ends. After the birth of a girl, the entire formula is multiplied by two. The initial period of seven days doubles and becomes fourteen days. Then, the mother counts an additional sixty-six days before she can go up to the Beis Hamikdash with her *korban*.

A superficial understanding of these laws of the Torah would lead a person to conclude that boys are somehow superior or on a higher spiritual level than girls. After all, girls produce twice the amount of *tumah*. But that would indeed be a shallow reading of the Torah.

Perhaps it would be better to begin by asking why the birth of any child, and particularly the arrival of a Jewish soul in the world, should produce any *tumah* in the first place.

The Kotzker Rebbe asks precisely this question, pointing out that Hashem Himself brings every soul into the world. If that is the case, there should be no place for *tumah* to be present at all. He answers enigmatically that actually the *tumah* comes *after* the birth.

The Shem Mi'Shmuel explains that this is analogous to the scientific principle that "nature abhors a vacuum." A vacuum is always replaced by something that rushes in to fill the space that has been vacated. In the spiritual world, too, when a pure soul emerges into the world, negative spiritual forces rush to occupy the space that the baby just vacated.

The process of purging that *tumah* takes twice as long for a girl as for a boy. The reason for this is that there is twice as much *kedushah* attached to a female soul than to a male soul. Consequently, after its departure from the womb, twice as much *tumah* fills the vacuum.

The same idea can be found with regard to the blessings we say every morning: *shelo asani goy*—"who has not made me a non-Jew"; *shelo asani aved*—"who has not made me a servant"; *shelo asani ishah*—"who has not made me a woman." Our obligation to say these blessings is codified in the *Shulchan Aruch* (*Orach Chaim* 46:4). The Bach asks an obvious question: Why not phrase these blessings positively? Instead of saying, *who has not made me a non-Jew*, for example, why not say *who has made me a Jew?*

He answers by citing a debate recorded in the Gemara (*Eruvin* 13b). Beis Shammai and Beis Hillel disagree concerning whether it was better for man to have been created or not. The Gemara's conclusion, and consequently the classic Jewish perspective on the question, is that it is better that we had never been created.

A very simple understanding of the conclusion of this two-and-a-half-year debate is that since man has been created and must therefore contend with the *yetzer hara*, there is a greater chance of getting things wrong than getting them right. In that case, we can't express the blessing in the positive, *who has made me a Jew*. From our perspective, it would have been better not to have been created at all—Jew or not, servant or not. Though every morning we are obliged to remind ourselves of our role in the world through the blessings, we can only express them in the negative: *who has not made me a non-Jew…a servant…a woman.*

Yet women say their blessing in a positive form: *she'asani kirtzono, who had made me according to His will.* The reason for this is that women quite simply have more of a chance of succeeding on their spiritual journey than men. In a sense, they have an easier time overcoming their *yetzer hara*. Had it been the wives of Beis Shammai and Beis Hillel conducting that debate, they would have likely reached a very different conclusion from that of their husbands.

In his *sefer Iyun Tefillah* (p. 45), Rav Shimon Schwab adds his perspective on the wording of the woman's blessing:

> In the morning blessing, women say, *Blessed are You, Hashem, our God, King of the universe, who has made me according to His will*. To understand the meaning of this blessing, we first have to understand the reason why women are not obligated to keep mitzvos whose observance is governed by time.
>
> Let us use the example of the mitzvah of *tefillin*, a time-bound mitzvah that women are not obligated to keep.
>
> All the mitzvos have one ultimate purpose, and that is to bring a person closer to Hakadosh Baruch Hu. This is made clear in the *pasuk*, *And it will be if you listen carefully to My mitzvos that I am commanding you this day…* (*Devarim* 11:13). The *pasuk* goes on to point out the purpose of heeding all the mitzvos: *…to love Hashem, your God*.
>
> Mitzvos are the vehicles for bringing a person to love and fear Hashem. Therefore, a Jewish man who refrains from observing even one mitzvah, such as *tefillin*, disconnects from Hashem by the amount of closeness to Hashem he would have achieved through that mitzvah. The absence of one mitzvah is an absence of the amount of connection to Hashem that it provides.
>
> This is the situation that governs a man's relationship with Hashem. Without the necessary ingredient of such mitzvos, he is unable to connect to his Creator.
>
> A woman, on the other hand, is not obligated to perform the mitzvah of *tefillin* simply because she is already able to become close to Hashem without it. This is the meaning of the blessing, *who has made me according to His will*. From the moment of her creation, she was made the way Hashem wanted. She doesn't need the mitzvah of *tefillin* or

other positive commandments to achieve attachment and connection to Him.

The same is true of the mitzvah of Torah study, a mitzvah in which a woman is also not obligated. True, women do say the blessing of *Birkas HaTorah*, because they are required to learn and know the mitzvos that they are obligated to carry out. But once they have mastered that knowledge, there is no requirement to learn Torah for its own sake. There is no need for them to create and strengthen a bond that already exists and is already strong.

A man, though, is obligated to learn the same piece of Gemara over and over, even 101 times. Even one of the greats of the generation, even someone who has the entire Torah at his fingertips, is still obligated to delve deeper and deeper and study the Torah both by day and by night.

It is simply not possible for a man to become God-fearing except by learning and struggling in Torah study.

This is not the case with women. They can even achieve prophecy, the ultimate level of connection between a human being and Hashem, without constant Torah study. The Gemara cites examples of precisely such women (*Megillah* 14a).

We have said that the purpose of mitzvos is to achieve love and fear of Hashem. A man who has spent his entire life studying Gemara without seeking a connection to Him will find that his learning is worthless. For him, the purpose of Torah study is precisely and solely to form that connection.

Conversely, were a woman to study Torah for that purpose, she would find she has not created or even added to her attachment to Hashem. That attachment already exists.

It is along similar lines that Rav Zalman Sorotzkin points to a woman's unique path in Torah by commenting on something surprising that occurred when Hashem offered the Torah to the Jewish people. The Torah tells us, *Moshe went up to God, and Hashem called to him from the mountain, saying, "This is what you shall say to* Beis Yaakov *and tell Bnei Yisrael"* (*Shemos* 19:3). In his *Oznayim LaTorah*, Rav Sorotzkin says:

"*Beis Yaakov*," the house of Yaakov, refers to the women. Why did Hashem speak to them first? Men are given a strong intellect, but women are created with deep feelings, which is the source from which faith is acquired. This is why it is clear that faith is stronger in women than in men, and this is why Hashem spoke to them first: the women would be easiest to convince, and they in turn would convince their husbands and children to accept the yoke of Torah and mitzvos.

This book explores the lives and choices of some of the greatest female figures in Tanach. Through the stories of these *nashim tzidkaniyos*, I will show precisely what the role of a Jewish woman is so that these special women can act as guides to those of us reading about them today. I have endeavored to see them afresh through the eyes of *Chazal* and other key sources that illuminate parts of their stories that are not well known or understood.

These stories demonstrate perfectly how the wives of Beis Shammai and Beis Hillel would have come to a different conclusion than their husbands if they had been asked whether it had been worthwhile for humans to have been created.

I will also introduce you to the stories of some of the daughters of these great women—women from more recent generations whose stories also touch us and give us examples to emulate. Some of these women are the wives of my teachers, *chavrusos*, and friends, and some are my *talmidos*. A glimpse into their lives demonstrates that Jewish women today remain very much in the mold of their mothers, following in their footsteps.

These are the stories of some of the great women of Klal Yisrael—then and now—showing us perfectly why women are known for their faith and devotion.

CHAPTER ONE

Sarah: Mother of the Jewish People

TO UNDERSTAND OUR mother Sarah, we need to consider exactly who she was and where she came from. This is especially important given that Rashi says that Avraham was not as great as Sarah in prophecy (*Bereishis* 21:12).

The clue to her greatness lies in the Torah's account of the ten generations from Adam to Noach and then the other ten from Noach to Avraham. The Kuzari points to the strangely repeating pattern of words when the Torah lists these generations. The generations start with Adam, as the Torah states:

> Adam lived 130 years, and he had a son in his likeness, and he called him Shes. The days of Adam's life after the birth of Shes were 800 years, and he had sons and daughters. The entire length of his life was 930 years, and he passed away.
>
> (*Bereishis* 5:3)

The pattern then repeats itself three *pesukim* later:

> Shes lived 105 years, and he had Enosh. The days of

Shes's life after the birth of Enosh were 807 years, and he had sons and daughters. The entire length of his life was 912 years, and he passed away.

And so it carries on through ten generations. In *Parshas Noach*, the pattern reemerges and repeats until the Torah comes to Avraham.

The Kuzari points out that even though the *pesukim* clearly state that Adam, Shes, Enosh, and all the others named among these ten generations lived very long lives and had *sons and daughters*, the Torah names only one son in each generation.

He explains that there was always one individual in each generation who was the next link in an unbroken line of prophets starting from the first prophet, Adam Harishon. This unbroken line brings us to the family of Avraham, who at that time was called Avram, and it includes his niece and wife, Sarah, who was then called Sarai (*Bereishis* 11:29).

An event then took place that is the next clue to the source of Sarah's prophetic greatness. The architect of that event was a wicked man called Nimrod—Avraham's nemesis.

Rebbetzin Tziporah Heller-Gottlieb often says in her *shiurim* that it is a mistake to view those who lived thousands of years ago as being less sophisticated than we are in our time. They may not have been as scientifically or technologically advanced as we are now—that is true. Their sophistication lay in other areas.

Through conquest and war, Nimrod built an empire. He had foreseen, through occult practices, that Avraham's arrival in the world was imminent. He was determined to prevent Avraham's stay here, or, rather, to make it very short lived. To that end, Nimrod issued a decree demanding that all male children should be killed at birth.

Avraham's mother, Amaslai bas Karnevo, tried to save her son and hid him in a cave until Nimrod's decree was rescinded. After that, it would be safe to send him to the yeshivah of Shem and Ever, which is precisely what happened.

Nimrod's first plan consequently failed, but he had a second and more ambitious one: He would enter into a conflict directly with Hashem! In Nimrod's world, as we explained, there was an unbroken line of prophets. Knowledge of Hashem was available to those who sought it. Nimrod planned to use that knowledge against its Creator. It was a strategy that Pharaoh would copy hundreds of years later.

Pharaoh knew that Hashem had promised never to bring another flood to the world after Noach's time. He knew that Hashem always punishes and rewards people for bad things they do *middah k'negged middah*—in the same way and measure that they did those things. If Pharaoh were to drown the Jewish babies, Hashem would be trapped by His own rules. He could not bring another flood, so the Egyptians would be safe from His retribution. He was nearly right, but he miscalculated. Hashem could not bring another flood to them, but He could bring *them* to a flood, and in the end, the Egyptians drowned in the Red Sea.

Nimrod acquired the knowledge that neither Avraham nor Sarah could have children, and *Chazal* confirm he was correct (*Yevamos* 64a). On the basis of this knowledge, Nimrod concluded that they didn't pose a real threat to him. No children meant no Klal Yisrael. Avraham and his followers would be a flash in the pan, soon to be forgotten. To make sure, though, that any future threat would be removed, he hatched a brilliant yet surprising plan. He audaciously conceived of creating an alternate Klal Yisrael!

He decided to unite the people of his generation, and this unity would mimic the essential ingredient that gives Klal Yisrael the ability to bring Heaven's blessings to the world and guarantee its survival.

Nimrod would take his "replica Klal Yisrael" further still. He ordered a mass migration to the west, to a valley called Shinar. There they would build a city with a tower that stretched to the heavens. Nimrod knew that for every positive thing in Hashem's world, there is an equal and opposite negative one. This allowed him to envisage that he could "checkmate" Hakadosh Baruch Hu with a move that was within the rulebook Hashem Himself had written.

They would build a city in the west to echo the one in the east called Yerushalayim. Yerushalayim is the point of contact between Heaven and Earth. It draws the energy the world needs to exist from above. The negative copy of the Holy City, too, would have a tower to mimic the Tower of David.

In Nimrod's time, the glue that bound the people of the world together and guaranteed their unity was the fact that they all spoke one language. This language was the first language, the one from which the world had been constructed. It was the one that Avraham's teacher Ever spoke and the one with which he taught Avraham. It was the language the first prophet, Adam Harishon, spoke. It was the language that Avraham would be known by—Avraham Ha'Ivri.

Nimrod's plan nearly succeeded. Hashem Himself declared, *They are one people with one language...nothing will be able to stop them* (*Bereishis* 11:6).

Nothing could stop them from becoming a negative copy of the Jewish people because they were unified. That unity flowed directly from their common language, so Hashem removed that from them. Their one language now became many languages. When human languages multiplied and misunderstanding became the norm, their unity evaporated.

Some unique individuals, students and followers of the unbroken line of prophets that stretched back to Adam, did not have the essential language taken from them. One of the families that retained it was Avraham's family. It was the language his mother (who was also Sarah's grandmother), Amaslai bas Karnevo, spoke.

Now we can begin to understand how Sarah could come to walk the path that would lead her to become a prophetess even greater than her husband. As part of an unbroken line of prophets beginning with Adam Harishon, Sarah spoke the language of her family, a language that was the key to fully unlocking the knowledge of Hashem that leads to prophecy.

CHAPTER TWO

Sarah: Greater than Avraham

NOW THAT WE know how Sarah came to prophecy, let's try to understand the source of Sarah's greatness, in which she was considered greater than Avraham Avinu. To bring us to this understanding, Rav Dessler takes us further into Sarah's journey:

> Before the Torah was given at Sinai, it resided in Heaven, and it was unattainable except by those who stage by stage reached the highest spiritual levels. Such a person would discover the Torah within his or her own pure soul. This is what the Midrash means when it says, *From where did Avraham Avinu learn Torah? Hashem prepared his kidneys to act like two rabbis, and they revealed the Torah to him* (*Bereishis Rabbah* 1:1).
>
> (*Michtav Me'Eliyahu*, vol. 3, p. 223)

This baffling statement needs elucidation, and that clarity can be found in Rav Dessler's explanation of the reference to the kidneys in the statement he quotes from the Midrash. He says that kidneys are mentioned in the *pasuk, Hashem examines the heart and the kidneys* (*Yirmiyahu* 11:20). Rav Dessler goes on to explain:

> The intellect alone is insufficient to show a person the truth. Truth will always be influenced by the heart's desires. Those desires will distort the truth and lead him to a conclusion that allows those very desires… The process of allowing your heart to bend the truth to the conclusion you desire is one that we are often unaware of ourselves. It is, in fact, a subconscious form of self-delusion. The metaphor for this process of self-delusion is the kidneys, and it is this part of the body that Hashem examines as well as a person's heart.
>
> (*Michtav Me'Eliyahu*, vol. 2, p. 36)

The kidneys are a perfect metaphor for the process of self-delusion since they are hidden and, unlike a beating heart or expanding lungs, are silent within the human body. Hashem looks to see how much pretense and self-delusion we engaged in that enabled us to ignore the role our heart and its desires played in bringing us to the various conclusions we reached throughout our lives.

When Avraham set out on his spiritual journey, he was able to reach pre-Torah spiritual heights precisely because he confronted his own predisposition to allow his heart to dominate the truth. He also confronted his human nature of pretending that very process did not occur. As Rav Dessler states elsewhere, *The* yetzer hara *is never given the ability to conceal the truth completely* (*Michtav Me'Eliyahu*, vol. 1, p. 60). Each person is capable of looking into his or her heart and seeing the truth in it—if they choose to look. Avraham chose to look.

We will soon see that women naturally engage in this process of pretense and self-delusion far less than men, but before we discuss why this is so, let's return to Rav Dessler and his insight concerning how people accessed Torah before it was revealed and brought down to earth at Mount Sinai:

> Someone who has climbed to that level of self-awareness and has purified his or her soul will discover the Torah [which they were already taught before they came into this world] within themselves.
>
> (*Michtav Me'Eliyahu*, vol. 2, p. 40)

Sarah embarked on the same journey of self-awareness and self-discovery as Avraham. It was a journey that led to knowledge of Hashem and direct communication with Him.

We now have a second key to unlocking the mystery of how Sarah was able to achieve a level of prophecy. We still have to understand how she reached a greater level than that of Avraham.

Rav Shimon Schwab provides a truly brilliant insight into Sarah's greatness, ironically by examining the one incident that led Hashem to criticize her.

The Torah tells us that when Sarah heard that she would give birth to a child at the age of ninety, she laughed. The *pasuk* then states, *Hashem said to Avraham, "Why did Sarah laugh?...Is anything impossible for Hashem?" And Sarah denied it, saying, "I did not laugh," because she was afraid, and He said, "No, but you laughed"* (*Bereishis* 18:13–15). The Midrash comments:

> Hashem only once spoke directly to a woman, and it was to the saintly Sarah. Even then, it was only after she was positioned into denying that she had laughed. Hashem engineered many circumstances to bring her to this denial and to Him speaking to her.
>
> (*Bereishis Rabbah* 48:20)

Rav Dessler explains that Sarah didn't realize that she had laughed, that it only occurred at the subconscious level. In any case, if she was worthy of Hashem speaking to her, why did He communicate with her only through an angel until then? And why did He place so many hurdles before her and only then spoke to her?

To answer this question, we turn to the Gemara, which relays a strange story:

> Caesar once said to Rabbi Yehoshua ben Chananiah, "I would like to see your God."
>
> Rabbi Yehoshua replied, "It is not possible to see Him."
>
> Caesar persisted and said to Rabbi Yehoshua, "I truly want to see Him."
>
> Rabbi Yehoshua promised to take Caesar out at midday

at the height of the summer when he said he could see Him. When he did so, he instructed Caesar, "Look at the sun."

Caesar replied, "I could not possibly do that!"

Rabbi Yehoshua said, "If it is impossible to look at one of God's servants for the briefest of times, how much more so is it impossible to look at Hashem Himself!"

(*Chullin* 59b)

Caesar was not so foolish that he would suppose that he could look at Hashem with his corporeal eyes. What he wanted to know was whether he could glimpse Hashem's essence and perceive His being. Rabbi Yehoshua's response was to point out that the human eye can't gaze at the sun because so much light would overwhelm and destroy it. If a finite human mind were to try to perceive the infinite—the *Ein Sof*—it would similarly be destroyed.

There is, however, a way for the human eye to look at the sun without being damaged, and that is to use the filter of a heavily darkened lens that blocks too much light from getting through. The same is true of a human mind perceiving Hashem's essence. The experience would have to be filtered to limit the amount of insight the brain receives so that it is exposed only to the amount it can take.

This is why Hashem never speaks directly to women. A woman's fundamental nature offers far less resistance to the spiritual than a man's. Denied the natural barrier and automatic resistance that men have to that which is spiritual, she would absorb too much and be destroyed by it.

Hashem had to manipulate circumstances in order to orchestrate the first-ever exception to the rule of not speaking to women directly (according to this explanation, other prophetesses received prophecy only through an angel). He had to arrange for Sarah to adopt a male position—to resist, refute, and "block" Him, which she did when she said, *I didn't laugh*. With that filter in place, Hashem could then speak to her directly. (Beforehand, she was able to prophesy, but she was not able to receive a direct communication from Hashem.)

We have now arrived at the most fundamental element that led Sarah to outshine her husband. They both came from identical backgrounds and had identical access to the unbroken chain of prophecy. They both were able to access the process of self-refinement that tradition taught and elevate themselves through it. But Sarah had one advantage over her husband that he could never have: She was a woman. This created a natural advantage, concerning which the Rambam elaborates in precise detail which factors are required for any human being to attain prophecy:

> Prophecy is bestowed only on someone who possesses outstanding wisdom. He must have completely mastered his character. His *yetzer hara* must never be able to master him; rather, he must consciously and constantly master it. He must possess a wide range of knowledge at the deepest and most accurate level. He must be physically sound, and when he enters the Pardes [the repository for mystical and esoteric wisdom] and draws from those sublime and abstract concepts, he will have developed the capability of understanding and absorbing them. In turn, he will become holy and will advance and become disconnected from the perspective of most human beings and their preoccupation with the fleeting ephemeral concerns of their times… Such a person's mind and thoughts will be solely connected to Heaven, being focused on heavenly realities and perspectives…
>
> (*Hilchos Yesodei HaTorah* 7:1)

The greatest barrier that separates any human being from Hashem is the sense of self and ego. The focus on the "I" inevitably disconnects us from Hakadosh Baruch Hu and causes our wants to conflict with His.

Women have a lesser sense of self than men. This, of course, is essential because it allows them to focus on their children and place them before their own needs. If a child has to nurse, a woman's nature is to stop whatever she is doing or wants to do and feed her child. The female nature automatically makes space for others. This facility flows from being endowed with a smaller sense of self and allows women to more easily attain the Rambam's conditions for achieving prophecy.

The best example of this essential characteristic of feminine spirituality is actually Moshe Rabbeinu. His humility was the antidote to his sense of self. With that barrier reduced beyond what any human had previously achieved, he became closer to Hashem than any other human being possibly could. Thus the *pasuk* states, *All honor of the King's daughter is within* (*Tehillim* 45:14). The daughter of the king referred to here is Moshe. When he prepared the Mishkan for Hashem's arrival and was on the most sublime spiritual level, he is referred to in the feminine form.

The same message is conveyed earlier in *pasuk* 10 when it refers to the *daughters of the king*. These, the Alshich explains, are the tzaddikim of the generations. So the greatest of Klal Yisrael, too, are referred to in the feminine.

These references all hint at the idea that the eradication of the sense of self, of the ego, is essentially a female trait. When it is attained, it is expressed in the feminine form. Moshe is the *daughter* of the King, not His son.

We have now established that the combination of Sarah's background and her nature equipped her for the journey she would take with her husband. The *Zohar* takes us even further back in the story of this most remarkable person—to the first Jewish woman. In so doing, we come to two themes to which we will return in our discussions of many of the Jewish women in this book: their names and their *gilgulim*, their previous lives.

Sarah would undergo many changes through her 127 years in this world. The major junctions of change were marked when her name was changed from Sarai to Yiskah (a name that denotes her ability to prophesy—see *Bereishis* 11:29 and *Rashi* there) and then to Sarah. But the *Zohar* says she was once known by another name entirely: She was once called Chavah, and Avraham was once called Adam.

In their first incarnation, they made the earth-shattering mistake of eating from the *eitz hada'as*. Their souls were brought to the world a second time in order to repair the damage they wrought and start the work of restoring the world to the way Hashem wanted it to be.

Now that we know the backdrop of Sarah's life and how she achieved such greatness, let us see how she applied her unique traits to overcome the challenges she faced on her life's journey.

CHAPTER THREE

Sarah: Her Journeys and Tests

THE *PARSHIYOS* IN the Torah about Avraham and Sarah contain her challenges and tests in the same way they contain those of her husband. They were, after all, two parts of the same soul, and, as we said at the end of the previous chapter, they shared the same mission.

Avraham welcomed kings and nobles into his tent and soon afterward introduced them to belief in Hashem. Sarah performed precisely the same role for women, welcoming queens and princesses into her tent. Of course, if you can convince a king and queen to change their beliefs, their people are likely to follow. Avraham was the embodiment of *chessed*, but so was Sarah; they were, after all, one soul.

They both faced tests that would set the stage for similar ones that their children would one day face. In passing them, they created the potential within their children to pass their tests, too. They suffered famine in their land and had to flee to Egypt, and so, too, would Yaakov and his family. Pharaoh wanted to take Sarah as a wife and would have been more than happy to kill her husband. His successor wanted to save the girls who were born and kill the boys. The Pharaoh in Sarah's time was punished with disease, and so later, just before the Exodus, was his successor and his people during the ten plagues.

Every aspect of Avraham and Sarah's life became the blueprint or, more accurately, the prototype that their children could use when they experienced similar circumstances. As the Midrash puts it, *Everything that happened to the* Avos *was a blueprint for their children* (*Tanchuma, Lech Lecha* 9).

Eventually came the miraculous arrival of a son called Yitzchak when Sarah was ninety years of age. Some people were skeptical, and cynics whispered that it was really some younger woman's child. How could anyone give birth at such an advanced age? So Sarah nursed the babies of those who came to visit. That is how they knew that she had indeed given birth.

One of Sarah's tests recorded in *Lech Lecha* troubled me greatly—the one that involved Hagar. The Torah tells us that after Hagar conceived, *Her mistress [Sarah] became diminished in her eyes* (*Bereishis* 16:4). Rashi comments, *Hagar said, "Sarah's conduct in secret is not like her conduct in public. She appears to be a righteous woman, but she is not a righteous woman, for she did not merit to conceive all these years."*

Hagar offered evidence to support her claim: As soon as she married Avraham, she was immediately blessed with a child. Sarah had been denied that blessing even after many decades as Avraham's wife.

Here was another accusation that would have excited the interests of cynics and skeptics. Its reasoning did contain a certain logic. It must have been convincing to many who heard it. After all, Hagar was no simple servant of Sarah. She had the same relationship with her mistress as Eliezer had with Avraham. Both were their closest and greatest *talmidim*.

Then, there was the question of Sarah's reaction and her demand that Hagar should be expelled from the household. This hardly fits with her reputation as the queen of *chessed*!

According to Rav Yitzchak Eizik Sher of Slabodka (*Leket Sichos Mussar*, p. 46), the real story was actually very different from the one the world thinks it knows.

Hagar's immediate pregnancy led to her loosening her dedication to her teacher's path and approach. It caused her sense of "I," her ego, to grow. It led her to see herself as the superior of the two. The pupil had "overtaken" the teacher. Yet this provoked no reaction from Sarah. In fact, she still encouraged her *talmidos* to go and visit Hagar. Kind acts to someone who is attacking you can sometimes stop the attack more effectively than hitting back.

Rav Sher explains that Sarah only reacted strongly when Hagar started saying her own Torah and teaching her own insights.

A chassid models his life on that of his rebbe. He usually dresses like him, behaves like him, and, crucially, *thinks* like him. It would be impossible for any ordinary person to detect the tiny nuance that Hagar introduced from her own perspective as opposed to repeating what she heard from Sarah. That tiny, alien, and anathematic idea could grow and metastasize into something that might one day poison and subvert everything Sarah taught. And as we have seen, Sarah's teachings were ideas inspired by Heaven. They came to her lips through prophecy. Hagar's anathematic ideas could grow into something that might one day subvert Torah.

Sarah had to act to protect the truth about Hashem's Torah. The question that always troubled me was: Why didn't she act to protect the truth about herself?

There are few people reading this who will not have experienced their own "Hagar" in their life—or perhaps several. Having people spread lies or half-truths about us hurts. It must have hurt Sarah Imeinu, too.

My *rosh yeshivah*, Rav Leib Lopian, once told me many years ago (when I experienced my first serious "Hagar" incident), "If you are going to spend your life worrying about what people are going to say about you, you will never succeed."

Of course, Rav Leib was well aware of the mishnah that says that the "crown" of a good name is above all other crowns (*Avos* 4:17) and the one that says, *If the spirit of people are pleased with someone, the spirit of Hashem will be, too* (*Avos* 3:13). Both those definitions applied perfectly to Sarah, yet despite that, she had Hagar slandering her and trying to tear her down. Rav Leib's message to me was that despite the Hagars in our lives, we can still achieve greatness.

Rav Dessler addresses this very issue where he discusses receiving *kavod* from others:

What does a person gain if he is considered important in the eyes of others? Only if a person is actually worthy of it does he earn true *kavod*, no matter what others think. If he is worthy, the estimation and approbation of others is irrelevant.

(*Michtav Me'Eliyahu*, vol. 1, p. 99)

Sarah Imeinu was well aware of this Torah truth. Her continued growth to the point where she would have her own child was not diverted or distracted by what others thought of her. She directed her journey solely by what Hashem thought of her.

I recall my *rosh kollel*, Rav Boruch Rapaport *shlit"a*, telling me of an incident that happened to his father, Dayan Avraham Rapaport *zt"l*, of the London Beis Din. A certain individual, although he had once been a *talmid chacham*, had become an *apikorus*. The *beis din* opposed his appointment to a key rabbinic position. The largest UK Jewish newspaper, which is Reform, called the *dayan* for quotes. He always gave the same reply: "No comment." That didn't stop this particular publication from making up quotes and attributing them to the *dayan* anyway.

Dayan Rapaport's wife used to get very upset and tell her husband to "fight back." He would reply, "No matter what the other person says or does, I have to be able to look at myself in the mirror and say, '*I* was a mensch…*I* did the right thing."

That's perfect advice for anyone when he comes across the Hagars in life. It was the constant compass that steered Sarah's journey and directed how she dealt with her tests.

CHAPTER FOUR

Rebbetzin Miriam Salomon

THERE ARE TWO well-known touchstones that identify a Torah life and the Torah's prerequisite for *kedushah* to exist among the Jewish people. Both have particular relevance to women.

The first is found in the *pasuk*, *Kol kevudah bas melech penimah*—"All honor of the King's daughter is within" (*Tehillim* 45:14). The entire honor of the daughter of the King is her *tznius*, her modesty (*Rashi*).

The second is found in the second *pasuk* of *Parshas Kedoshim*: *Speak to the entire congregation of Bnei Yisrael and say to them, "You will be holy because I, Hashem, your God, am holy."* Rashi comments, *To be holy means to separate yourself from immorality, for in every place that you find barriers erected to guard against immorality, there you will find holiness.*

As anyone reading these pages knows, our communities throughout the world, from Eretz Yisrael to Los Angeles to Melbourne, have these two principles woven into every inch of their everyday life.

Women typically don't want fanfare and kudos for their *avodas Hashem*; in fact, they usually flee from it. Yet at the *hespedim* in Lakewood's Beth Medrash Govoha for Rebbetzin Miriam Salomon *a"h*, the *roshei yeshivah*, Rav Malkiel Kotler, Rav Yerucham Olshin, and Rav Dovid Schustal, spoke with emotion and firsthand knowledge of the remarkable achievements of someone whose name was synonymous with the principle conveyed by, *All honor of the King's daughter is within.*

I once taught at a Shavuos assembly in a certain seminary, and I quoted *Chazal*, who say that someone who runs after *kavod*, honor, will find that it flees from him, while those who run away from *kavod* will find that it chases after them (*Eruvin* 13b).

One of my *talmidos* once asked, "So it would seem to make no difference whether you are running after *kavod* or from it—you will always remain the same distance from it!"

Then she added a brilliant insight: "No…there actually *is* a difference. When you grow old, you slow down!"

If you've been running after *kavod*, you slow down as you get older, so *kavod* gets further and further away from you. But if you've been fleeing from *kavod* your entire life, as you get older, it will catch up to you.

It seems that eventually the edifice of *chessed*, *avodah*, and Torah that Rebbetzin Salomon built simply grew too large to conceal. No matter how much such a *bas Melech* may try to hide what she does, everyone, man and woman, can't fail to notice how widespread it has grown and how high it has reached.

I am very lucky. Rav Matisyahu Salomon *shlit"a* has been my *rebbi* and guide since I was a *bachur* in Gateshead Yeshivah many decades ago. I knew of the Rebbetzin's *chessed* from then. I also had the enormous privilege of knowing her parents. For those whose eyes were open and wanted to see special and unique individuals, Rebbetzin Salomon's parents, Reb Avraham Tzvi and Mrs. Sarah Falk, were a treasure to be discovered.

The lives of the truly great are rarely revealed to others by one enormous dramatic event or episode. The realization that they are simply of an entirely different quality from most of us emerges slowly over time as we grow close to them. Discovering such greatness is made further difficult by the fact that *All honor of the King's daughter is within* is an ideal to which both women *and* men aspire. Great people seek Hashem's recognition and approval, not other people's. That means that Klal Yisrael's *gedolim* often appear simple and ordinary while being anything but.

I have written in two of my other books about my many conversations with Mr. Falk and how he fortified me by telling me the story of the train journey that took him to Buchenwald. "It was a place," he said, "that took people and ground them into tiny bits!"

It did not grind Mr. Falk into bits. He collected the water that ran down the wall beside his bed every night for *negel vasser* in the morning. He organized *shiurim* for the other prisoners. I heard a hint in something he let slip once that said he did much more, but Klal Yisrael's *gedolim* don't easily share what they do.

He was somehow released from that deadly place and reached England shortly before war was declared. There he met his wife, Sarah Kleyva, who had arrived in England from Hamburg. The couple settled in Manchester, and even by the standards of postwar hardship, they were noticeably poor. A glimpse of that hardship was shared when Rebbetzin Salomon's brother, Rav Pesach Eliyahu Falk *zt"l*, another of my teachers, passed away. His son said, "My father did not sleep in a normal bed until he was fifteen. Before then, his bed consisted of orange crates with a mattress on top." Rebbetzin Salomon told my wife that her parents were only able to give her a new dress when she was ten years old. She recalled how overjoyed she was at reaching such a milestone in her life.

Mr. Falk was meticulous and kept a careful record of every penny he borrowed while establishing himself in a new country. Only when every single penny was repaid did he allow himself to grow his beard long. He felt that wearing the full beard of an Orthodox Jew while owing people money was not appropriate.

(An interesting footnote: Mr. and Mrs. Falk were leading members of the "mother shul" of all *chareidi* synagogues in Manchester, Machzikei Hadas, which was founded in 1925. It was constructed on the site of a building that had previously been owned by the British Union of Fascists and had served as their northern headquarters. The British Nazis were being harassed by the British government and were desperate for cash. They decided to sell their property to raise funds. The *kehillah* knew that these Nazis would not sell to Jews, so a proxy was found, and the purchase went through. When Sir Oswald Mosley, *yemach shemo*, the British Hitler, learned what had transpired, he tried to back out of the sale but was legally unable to do so. The Falk family, along with the many other Machzikei Hadas refugee victims of Hitler, must have smiled when they heard the story.)

The Falks were determined that their children should all marry or become *bnei Torah*. When Rav Matisyahu Salomon was suggested as a *shidduch* for their daughter, many thought the suggestion was ridiculous and the Falks were mad for enthusiastically accepting it. In those postwar days, most felt they had to put their efforts into securing financial security and finding sons-in-law who shared that ambition. Rav Matisyahu was one of the elite who gained entry into the Gateshead Kollel founded by Rav Dessler. This meant that the life of poverty that Rebbetzin Salomon knew as a girl continued as she established her own home as a young woman.

A childhood in which material ambitions and possessions were foreign was simultaneously one in which *ruchniyus*, *chessed*, and Torah were abundant. The same values seamlessly traveled with her from Manchester in England's northwest to Gateshead in its northeast.

As one of Rav Matisyahu's *talmidim*, I am able to share a tiny glimpse of what it must have meant to be married to Rav Matisyahu at that time. When I entered Gateshead Yeshivah, Rav Matisyahu was serving as junior *mashgiach* of the yeshivah (Rav Moshe Schwab was the senior *mashgiach*), and I attended many of his *shiurim* during my period as a *bachur* and then a *yungerman* there. Like all *talmidim*, I got to know my *rebbi's* schedule very well. There were scores of *shiurim*, *chaburos*, and *va'adim* every week, and, of course, many hours were set aside for counseling *bachurim*, married *talmidim*, and couples.

I was also very friendly with Rav Matisyahu's oldest brother, Reb Yosef *zt"l*. He owned and ran Gateshead's Kosher Dairy, the sole supplier of milk to the entire community. One day, he approached me and asked if I would like to become his "deputy," stepping in when he was out of town at a *simchah* in London and the like. This required getting up at four o'clock in the morning and driving to the farm where the cows were milked some forty minutes away in Sunderland.

I happily agreed and went with him that day to see exactly what was involved. That night, Reb Yosef parked the van outside my house so it would be waiting for me to drive it to the farm in the morning. He posted the van keys plus a list of my instructions through the mailbox. The first instruction read, "Wake up at 4 a.m." The second instruction said, "Phone Rav Matisyahu"!

Reb Yosef called his brother at that time every morning to wake him up. Since he was so busy with his duties teaching and helping others all day long, this was the time he rose to learn for himself.

Rebbetzin Salomon told my late wife *a"h* that midnight was the time her husband started to see the young marrieds in the *kehillah* who came to him for guidance. "If he went to bed before two o'clock in the morning, that was a good night," she said.

Besides his two hours of sleep at night, Rav Matisyahu also slept for an hour around midday, so if he had more than three hours of sleep in a day, that was unusual. Sharing a husband and so much of his time and life with so many others would be an impossible task for most women. And when the Salomons moved to Lakewood, and his status as one of the *gedolei hador* became clear, the Rebbetzin's workload expanded enormously to facilitate his.

Before I moved to New York from England, I stayed with the Salomons often whenever I traveled to the U.S. to give *shiurim*, and one of my sons stayed with them when he learned in Beth Medrash Govoha. Rebbetzin Salomon's smile was always there to greet me when I came back from each *shiur*. She would inquire how it had gone, and inevitably, the rather complicated and sophisticated phone that sat on her kitchen table interrupted us over and over again. This was the portal that people from all over the world went through to reach her husband. It was insistent and relentless.

The phone would ring, and the Rebbetzin would say, "Salomon" and then quickly consult her notebook. Some of the calls came from other *gedolim*. Many were calls from Rav Matisyahu's *talmidim* or from the Rebbetzin's *talmidos* to share good news and *simchos*. Most, though, were from people calling from all over the world—from Lakewood, Gateshead, Brooklyn, Los Angeles, Australia, Russia, and, naturally, Eretz Yisrael—who were desperate for help and guidance, who were facing challenges and crises. Rebbetzin Salomon listened and assessed them all. Naturally, everyone thinks *his* problem is urgent, and the Rebbetzin had to listen and evaluate who needed to speak to her husband as soon as possible and who could wait a day or maybe more.

Occasionally, she would look at the notes she had made and realize that she had forgotten to find someone an appointment. Her look of regret and remorse was instantaneous as she struggled to remedy her mistake and squeeze the person in.

Once or twice after the *petirah* of my first wife and my remarriage, my wife and I would be sitting at that kitchen table, and we saw the Rebbetzin looking overwhelmed. On one occasion, she was about to leave to go to a *simchah* when someone called, and the Rebbetzin realized that she had forgotten to find them an appointment. She became so distressed. After a few moments, she regained her composure, solved the problem, and moved on.

I paused before writing about this incident. Some believe in editing ordinary human emotions and reactions out of stories of the lives of our *gedolim*. I don't believe that this story diminishes the Rebbetzin's greatness even the tiniest degree. In fact, to my mind, it demonstrates her greatness. Rebbetzin Salomon was not unlike an air traffic controller at JFK Airport or London's Heathrow Airport, deciding which plane arrives at the right time and in the right place. The difference was that *all* the planes wanted to arrive at the same time and on the same runway—and no other air traffic controllers had turned up for work that day!

Her role was simply enormous, as was the burden she carried. As Rav Matisyahu said at her *levayah*, he relied *entirely* on her. It was not an easy responsibility, and if it was, carrying it out would not have shown her total commitment to her husband's critical role in Klal Yisrael. It would not have shown how she continued to live up to the values she learned in her parents' home in Manchester, where *ruchniyus*, *chessed*, and Torah were so abundant.

All of this took place while she was surrounded by her many children and grandchildren, who seemed to so often fill her kitchen and help her prepare for a *sheva brachos*, Yom Tov, or Shabbos.

That was the other thing about Rebbetzin Miriam Salomon: She built her edifice of Torah, which kept growing wider and taller, while all the time building her family so that they grew in that way, too.

For many years, her health was not good. She suffered heart problems, and walking was a challenge. I recall one time when she was admitted to the hospital, and the doctors' prognosis was grim. I remember Rav Matisyahu's words to my late wife when she received an equally grim prognosis from her doctors. He phoned her at the hospital and told her, "A doctor told you that you don't have long to live? A doctor? Don't forget who you are! Hashem decides these matters, not doctors."

My wife left her hospital bed to return home to her family around the same day they predicted would be her last. Rebbetzin Salomon left her hospital bed, too, and returned to her home on Lakewood's Sixth Street. When she arrived home, some of her children, grandchildren, and great-grandchildren stood outside waiting for her. I recall seeing a picture of that large crowd, her family excitedly anticipating her arrival. So, too, was the rest of Klal Yisrael, and very soon, she was back at her kitchen table and the flashing lights of her phone. Once again, she was directing the most urgent calls, telling the callers when they could "land" and the less urgent ones that they would be in a holding pattern for a little longer.

As my wife and I are both in a second marriage, many people in our situation seek our advice on how to overcome the inevitable difficulties that arise the second time around. One such couple were really struggling, and we arranged for them to meet with Rebbetzin Salomon and her husband.

We joined in the meeting. It was a rare opportunity to observe the interaction between the Rav and the Rebbetzin.

You may have seen for yourself that an older couple who have been married for a long time do not seem to need to communicate verbally at all. They seem to know exactly what the other is thinking before they express it. That was what we saw that night. Both had total respect for each other's thoughts and views. In fact, there was no difference between them. They both spoke, but truly either could have said the words of the other, so seamlessly were they in harmony.

That couple was only the latest of thousands who had visited the Salomons for couples' counseling. Over the years, I saw so many others who made their way to Sixth Street with various problems. In fact, *every* kind of problem. Some were invited to stay for a while and become part of the family. I saw people there suffering from depression or other forms of mental illness. The Salomon home became their refuge, a safe place where they could recover and heal.

The Salomon home might just as easily contain another *gadol* who was visiting to spend a day consulting with Rav Matisyahu and discussing urgent matters of the day affecting Klal Yisrael. News of the illustrious visitor's presence may have spread through the town, causing *bachurim* to gather, hoping to catch a glimpse of the *gadol*. At the same time, there might well be some other Jewish soul staying in the Salomon house who would have attracted no such interest. He or she may have lost their home or perhaps their way and were being helped and encouraged to find the way back to standing on their own feet. And there were often Jews visiting from out of town, recent *talmidim* or older ones like me who simply wanted the *chizuk* of being with the *mashgiach* and his *rebbetzin*.

There was no form of *chessed* that didn't take place in the Salomon home. Elul in particular found the Rebbetzin sitting under piles of envelopes containing funds for one of the many *tzedakah* causes she helped.

After the Rebbetzin's *petirah*, I went to visit Rav Matisyahu and the other *aveilim* during the *shivah*, and someone who had come from Gateshead recalled a story that left the hundreds of people who were squeezed into the room amazed.

One day in Gateshead, Rebbetzin Salomon heard the front doorbell ring. When she opened it, there was a young girl standing there holding a baby. Her mother had given birth a few weeks before and needed to return to the hospital for treatment. She had no one to watch the baby and had told her daughter to take the baby girl to Rebbetzin Salomon, assuming the Rebbetzin would look after the baby until the mother's return.

"Tell your mother that it's no problem," she said, taking the baby in her arms. She then walked upstairs to her bedroom, where she lay the baby on the bed. Then, she opened one of the drawers in her dresser and emptied out all the contents.

The Rebbetzin folded a sheet to make a mattress and carefully placed the baby in her new crib. When the newborn became hungry and started to cry, Rebbetzin Salomon, who had just had her own baby at that time, nursed this baby, too. Eventually the mother came home and collected her child. The baby girl grew up, married a *ben Torah*, and settled in Lakewood.

Years later, one of Rebbetzin Salomon's granddaughters became unwell and was unable to nurse her own baby. There is a *gemach* in Lakewood for mother's milk, which is frozen and kept for babies whose mothers aren't able to nurse. Rebbetzin Salomon's granddaughter was able to access the services of this organization to provide the milk her baby needed.

One of the women who donated milk to the *gemach* that fed Rebbetzin Salomon's grandchild was a young Jewish woman from Gateshead who had settled in Lakewood. As a baby, when *her* mother had been unwell and unable to nurse her, she had been nursed by Rebbetzin Salomon. That train of *chessed* that the Rebbetzin had set in motion traveled through generations. It was in a sense almost as though Rebbetzin Salomon was nursing her own great-granddaughter decades later.

As mentioned above, *Chazal* say that when Sarah Imeinu gave birth to Yitzchak, all the women brought their babies to be nursed by her. In a tent filled with *chessed*, such a request would inevitably be fulfilled.

As Avraham and Sarah's tent traveled from place to place, it also traveled from time to time. You can see her tent pitched in many places through the long journey of her daughters and Klal Yisrael. You could see it very clearly, too, not long ago, in Gateshead's Windermere Street and Lakewood's Sixth Street.

CHAPTER FIVE

Rivkah: Stepping into Sarah's Shoes

IMMEDIATELY AFTER THE account of the *Akeidah*, the Torah informs us about Avraham's family. His brother Nachor's oldest son was called Utz. Utz had a brother called Buz and six others. Eventually, the explanation of the family tree reaches Besuel, Rivkah's father. Rashi says that the Torah delineates the entire family tree only in order to announce the birth of the woman who would marry Avraham's son.

Rashi's comment may leave you wondering why this is necessary. Why not simply inform us of Rivkah's birth and omit all the others?

The Ohr Hachaim has a different explanation (*Bereishis* 22:20). He states that there is a reason why the Torah tells about Nachor's family at this juncture. When the soul of a righteous person comes to this world, especially one such as Rivkah's, whose soul was so holy despite the environment in which she grew up, an inevitable phenomenon occurs. Ever since Adam sinned, impurity always attaches itself to good. These negative forces manifest themselves in the birth of those souls that inevitably accompany the birth of any tzaddik when he or she comes into the world. By telling us about the other descendants of Nachor, the

Torah is indirectly praising Rivkah. Though she grew up with such corrupt people, she shone with all her virtues.

The twelve children of Nachor would be people Rivkah would encounter in her life and have to confront. They would present her with challenges in her early life that she would ultimately pass.

If someone were to ask you or me if we would like a father like Besuel or a brother like Lavan, the answer we would give is obvious. Yet Rashi tells us (*Bereishis* 25:20):

> She was the daughter of a wicked man and the sister of a
> wicked man, and she lived in a place surrounded by wicked
> people, but she did not [absorb their behavior and] learn
> from their deeds.

In this respect, Rivkah's life paralleled that of her son Yaakov, when he sent the message to his brother Esav that he had been living with their uncle Lavan. Rashi says that the phrase Yaakov employed in his message, Garti *(I lived) with Lavan,* meant "…*but* I have kept all 613 mitzvos" (the word "*garti*" has the same numerical value as "*taryag,*" 613).

Rav Yerucham Levovitz explains that Yaakov's message actually contained a much more profound message. Yaakov wasn't saying that he kept the 613 mitzvos *despite* living with Lavan. He kept them *because* he was living with him!

It is only when you are challenged and tested in life that you know whether you have mastered it. You can only know that you are faithful and scrupulous in keeping the Torah if you are presented with the invitation not to be. Lavan presented that challenge to Yaakov. The twelve souls that came to the world with that of Rivkah presented the same challenge and therefore the same opportunity.

After the death of Sarah, the next challenge Avraham faced was to secure possession of the Cave of Machpeilah as the family burial place. Thereafter, his task was making sure that Rivkah was brought from her home to be Yitzchak's bride.

We already mentioned that Avraham's family retained belief in Hashem and were adherents of an unbroken line of prophets. This is why Amaslai sent her son Avram to learn from Ever, Noach's grandson.

But that belief and attachment to the prophetic tradition and faith was much stronger in the female line than the male. For this reason, Avraham naturally looked there to select a wife for his son.

A glimpse of the contrast between the male and female members of Avraham's family is immediately apparent in the story of Eliezer's mission to bring Rivkah to Yitzchak. When Lavan realized that Avraham's servant was waiting outside, he ran to him and said, *Come, you who are blessed of Hashem. Why are you standing outside? I have cleaned out the house* (*Bereishis* 24:31).

Rashi explains this puzzling declaration, which seems to be Lavan saying that he was a good housekeeper, as actually meaning, "I have cleared away the idols from inside the house."

Lavan and his father understood that they should not allow a *talmid* of Avraham to see that they had idols in their home. That doesn't mean they thought they shouldn't have had them there in the first place.

We see that they were very far from anything related to prophecy, in direct contrast to their sister and daughter, Rivkah. The episode that led Eliezer to be standing outside Rivkah's home began when he asked Hashem for a sign that he was choosing the correct girl:

> Here I stand at the well, and the daughters of the city are coming to draw water. And it will be that the maiden to whom I say, "Lower your pitcher and I will drink," and she will say, "Drink, and I will also water your camels"—she is the one You have designated as the one for Your servant, for Yitzchak.
>
> (*Bereishis* 24:13–14)

But when Rivkah appeared at the well, something strange happened:

> She said, "Drink, my lord," and she hurried and lowered her pitcher in her hand and gave him to drink. Then she finished giving him to drink, and she said, "Also for your camels I will draw [water] until they are finished drinking."
>
> (*Bereishis* 24:18–19)

The Torah reports that Eliezer observed this young girl and her actions carefully to make sure that she fulfilled his conditions. Satisfied that she had, he gave her gifts of gold jewelry. But a careful reading of the story shows that Eliezer got it wrong! She did not do what he stipulated as the sign, after all. To explain why, we must first visit the words of Rav Dessler in an essay called "Refinement of Speech":

> There is huge importance attached to distancing yourself from crude forms of speech. I do not, of course, mean foul language and expressions, which are in any case forbidden. I am referring to expressing yourself in a refined way when saying things that are permissible.
>
> This point is expressed clearly in the Gemara (*Pesachim* 3a), which states, *The Torah added eight letters to avoid saying a less refined expression. It is written [regarding the animals that entered to Noach's ark], "From the animals that are pure you shall take for yourself seven pairs…and of the animals that are not pure, two…"* (*Bereishis* 7:2).
>
> The Torah could have said *tamei*, "impure," instead of *lo tehorah*, "not pure," but even though that would have been a more concise way of expressing the same idea, there was a better and more sensitive way to say the same thing so the Torah chose that way.
>
> The Gemara goes on to recount on the next page that two *talmidim* sat in front of Rebbi, and one of them was Rabbi Yochanan ben Zakkai. They were discussing a halachic point. One used the expression *lo tehorah* and the other said *tamei*. Rebbi declared, "I am certain that the one who avoided using the less delicate word will go on to teach Torah among Klal Yisrael." That prediction soon came true, and he became known as Rabbi Yochanan ben Zakkai.
>
> (*Michtav Me'Eliyahu*, vol. 4, p. 220)

In the chapter above, where we discussed Sarah and Hagar, we mentioned that Eliezer wasn't simply Avraham's servant. He was his greatest and most faithful *talmid*. At the end of his life, Avraham gave Eliezer permission to open his own yeshivah, where he faithfully taught his master's Torah. According to Rashi, Rivkah was three years old when Eliezer met her (other opinions say she was fourteen). Yet she had a level of refinement of speech that Avraham's lifelong *talmid* did not have.

Eliezer specified that the girl that Hashem had chosen should say to him, *Drink, and I will also water your camels.* What actually happened was that only after he finished drinking did she say, *Also for your camels I will draw water.* Rivkah understood that you don't speak about an animal and a human being in the same sentence.

Eliezer succeeded in bringing Rivkah with him to Yitzchak, and the three supernatural phenomena that had ceased with Sarah's passing suddenly and dramatically returned. Regarding these three phenomena, the Alshich states:

> The damage wrought by Adam and Chavah was greatly repaired by Avraham and Sarah. That process of repair was continued after them by Yitzchak and Rivkah.
>
> The *Zohar* says that all the *Avos* and *Imahos* were connected to Adam and Chavah through *gilgul*, reincarnation (*Vayechi*). That is why the *Avos* were buried alongside them [in the Cave of Machpeilah], and that is why the repair of the damage Chavah caused was signaled through three mitzvos: *niddah*, challah, and the Shabbos lights that perpetually burned. These three mitzvos relate to three of the four spiritual elements of a human being: *ruach*, *nefesh*, and the body. The fourth element, the *neshamah*, was not affected by Adam and Chavah's sin.
>
> Challah parallels the process that creates the physical body of a human being, which [like wheat] comes from the earth. Chavah's sin turned Adam's body from something completely pure and holy into something physical and mortal. Sarah's life acted to reverse that process. When she separated challah, the process produced something holy. And a miracle occurred: The dough expanded and lasted an entire week. This indicated that she has been successful in returning the physical state to a holy and pure one once more, separating the good from the bad.
>
> Death, which came to the world through Chavah's mistake, was also made to retreat through Sarah's life. This is hinted at by *niddah*.

Every occurrence of *niddah* happens when a potential life was never actualized and dies. Blood is identified with the *nefesh*: *For blood is the soul* (*Devarim* 12:23). When Chavah sinned, the *nefesh* was damaged. Sarah [who repaired that damage] had never been a *niddah* until just before she would conceive a child, Yitzchak. So essentially, she was not actually a *niddah* at all. The *Shechinah* resting above her tent [in the form of a cloud] signaled this. Thus, Sarah repaired the damage that the *nefesh* suffered.

The *ruach* of humanity [which symbolizes a person's light] was wounded by Chavah, too. That wound was referred to as a dimming of the light. This light that Chavah extinguished would be rekindled through Sarah, and that was shown through the miracle of the Shabbos lights that stayed lit all week.

Rivkah's arrival brought back the three miracles and demonstrated that she was able to carry on the process where Sarah left off. The process of repairing the damage to the world would now continue. Rivkah would take Sarah's place.

This shines a light on the words of the mishnah in the second paragraph of Shabbos, which state that women die in childbirth for one of three sins: for not being careful concerning *niddah*, challah, or lighting the Shabbos candles.

(Alshich, Bereishis 24:67)

The Alshich's last statement aligns with the Bartenura's classic explanation that childbirth is a life-threatening experience; therefore, a woman needs merits at this dangerous time. If she is lacking in these merits, she is truly in danger. (This similarly applies to men, of course, who also need merits when they find themselves in danger.) This insight from the Alshich tells us that these three specific threats to a woman in childbirth actually means that the amount of merit she gets at a time of danger will be measured against how much she has undone the effects of Chavah's original mistake, by how much she repairs the damage done to the three things that challah, *niddah*, and candle lighting represent.

For Rivkah, taking Sarah's role would mean more than simply carrying on her achievements. It would entail enduring her challenges, too. Like Sarah, Rivkah would struggle with childlessness. (The Gemara in *Yevamos* [64a] says that none of the *Imahos* were able to have children.) The Torah records that struggle:

> Yitzchak was forty years old when he took Rivkah, the daughter of Besuel the Aramean of Padan Aram, the sister of Lavan the Aramean, as a wife. Yitzchak pleaded with Hashem opposite his wife because she was barren, and Hashem accepted his prayer, and Rivkah his wife conceived.
>
> (*Bereishis* 25:20–21)

Both Rivkah and Yitzchak prayed for children, but Rashi notes that Hashem answered their pleas as a result of Yitzchak's prayer rather than Rivkah's:

> [Hashem accepted Yitzchak's prayers] but not hers, because the prayer of a tzaddik who is the child of a tzaddik does not compare to the prayers of a tzaddik who is the child of a *rasha*.

Regarding this statement of Rashi, Rav Yaakov Goldberg makes an important observation:

> It was only due to this principle that Yitzchak's prayers were answered over Rivkah's. Apart from that, their prayers were of equal value.
>
> We should pause and consider, at this stage in his life, how Yitzchak had embraced the test of the *Akeidah*. Now, at the age of sixty, he was at the height of his greatness and had instituted the prayer of Minchah as an inheritance for the Jewish people forever. Moreover, Yitzchak became one of the three *Avos* of the Jewish people. Yet with all that greatness, it was solely because his father was a tzaddik that his prayer had the edge over hers. In every other respect, they were equal in greatness.
>
> As Rashi says of Rivkah, her father was a wicked man, as was her brother, and so were the people among whom

she grew up, yet she did not allow herself to be affected by them in any way. This achievement then made her the equal of the man she would marry. Her challenges were considered the equivalent of everything he had undergone.

(Devir Kadsho)

This theme is echoed by the Alshich when he examines the first *pasuk* of *Parshas Toldos*: *Yitzchak was the son of Avraham; Avraham was the father of Yitzchak* (*Bereishis* 25:19).

Rashi's explanation for this puzzling repetition is that the scoffers and cynics of the generation sought to cast doubt on Yitzchak's parentage. They pointed out that Sarah had been married to Avraham for decades without being blessed with children. But soon after she was kidnapped by Avimelech, she had a child. Clearly, they claimed, Avimelech was Yitzchak's real father. To silence them, Hashem changed Yitzchak's face so that it would be a replica of Avraham's.

The Alshich isn't satisfied with Rashi's explanation. He points out that surely, then, Hashem would have changed Yitzchak's face to mirror his father's when he was born, not sixty years later.

But the reason that Hashem changed Yitzchak's appearance only now was because his prayer had been answered. And it produced not one child but two, and one was as unlike his parents as one could imagine. Now people wondered: How was it possible that Yitzchak and Rivkah could have produced an Esav? The old accusation about Yitzchak's paternity reemerged and was now reinvigorated. Hashem stamped it out with a miracle that changed Yitzchak's features.

The finger of blame now swung around to point at Rivkah. With a father and brother like hers, how could they not help but rub off on her? That would be a perfect explanation for Esav's arrival on the scene.

This, says the Alshich, is why the *pasuk* reports that Yitzchak pleaded with Hashem *l'nochach ishto*, which can be translated as "facing his wife." It was the fact that she was his wife and the perfect match for him that was the basis of his prayer and the case he made. It was the fact that she was indeed his equal that caused Hashem to endorse Yitzchak's prayer. Esav did not enter this world due to Rivkah any more than he did through Yitzchak. In fact, Esav was not fated to be wicked at all:

One thing is clear: Esav was not preordained to be a *rasha*. Even though there were many indicators before and after he was born that his nature inclined him in that direction, those were only indications of where his own personal battles would be fought and, if he chose, won.

(*Michtav Me'Eliyahu*, vol. 2, p. 205)

Esav was never fated to be a *rasha*, nor was it the fault of Yitzchak or Rivkah. That he was wicked was due to his own choices and his alone.

CHAPTER SIX

Rivkah: Like Sarah yet Not like Sarah

LTHOUGH THERE WERE many similarities between Rivkah's journey through life and Sarah's, there were many differences, too. Inevitably, just as Yitzchak's path differed from that of his father's, Rivkah's role as his wife would therefore have to be different from Sarah's role as Avraham's wife.

Everyone knows that marriages are made in Heaven, but people often forget that all marriages are made *differently* in Heaven. The formula that makes a marriage work is unique to each couple.

When Rivkah saw Yitzchak for the first time, she took her veil and covered her face (*Bereishis* 24:65). The *Hamek Davar* explains the reason for her action: Rivkah was in awe of Yitzchak and was even embarrassed to be in his presence. She didn't believe herself worthy of him. They were simply two completely different kinds of human beings. Yitzchak had, after all, been willing to offer himself as a sacrifice to Hashem. That perception remained with her throughout her life.

Rivkah's perspective led to a very different approach to dealing with her husband than that of Sarah. If Sarah disagreed with her husband, she had no hesitation in letting him know. Sarah was upset with

Avraham over Hagar and told him exactly what she expected him to do.

Rivkah's approach to her husband was born of the awe in which she held him, so she never openly challenged him and there was never a clash, even when she knew he was wrong.

The clearest example of this is that Rivkah knew that Yitzchak's plan to give the blessings to Esav was misguided and not what Hashem wanted. Her approach was to avoid it happening without a confrontation with her husband. She told her son what he must do instead of telling her husband what *he* must do.

Let us consider the idea of Hashem sending anyone a test. The issue is quite obvious. A test is designed to allow the examiner to know whether the person taking the test knows the material or is equipped enough to be qualified in a given task. But Hashem already knows the answer to that question before He tests anyone, so the actual question is, why does *He* need to test anyone?

This topic is obviously a vast one, but the Alshich offers several answers (*Bereishis* 22:1). For one thing, the test is not meant to let Hashem know whether the person can pass it; rather, the intention of the test is to let the person being tested know it. It affords the person the opportunity to discover something within himself that he didn't suspect was there. It's also possible that the intended audience for this discovery and revelation is other people who witness the person's triumph rather than the person being tested.

Another point for us to consider is the basic nature of any test. Unless it presents a difficulty and a challenge, it is not a test. You can demonstrate this right now by testing your basic mathematical abilities. See if you can answer this question: 1+1=?

That is clearly not a test for anyone reading this book. Instead, try answering the Poincaré conjecture in mathematics, the first conjecture ever made in topology. It was first posed in 1906 and was seen as one of mathematics' biggest unanswered questions. (It was finally solved in 2004.) If you could solve it, that would prove that you are an accomplished mathematician.

This leads the Alshich to explain why the *Akeidah* was a test for Avraham but not Yitzchak. It challenged Avraham, whose basic nature was kindness, to commit the ultimate act of cruelty and deny his nature. Yitzchak's nature, on the other hand, was total subservience to Hashem and His will. The request to offer his life for Hashem did not present him with a challenge and therefore could not, for him, be called a test.

Let us consider, given Rivkah's nature, what kind of test would challenge her—a test that demanded she honor her husband, whom she held in awe, or one that required her to defy and deceive that husband? The latter would certainly meet our definition of a test. She would have found that a huge challenge.

Of course, if Hashem told her to do it, that would make it easier. But it would still be a challenge. After all, Hashem commanded Avraham to kill his son, but it was still a challenge and a test.

Rivkah overheard Yitzchak telling Esav to prepare a meal in order to receive his blessing. She promptly turned to Yaakov and said, *And now, my son, listen* b'koli *(to my voice), to what I am commanding you* (*Bereishis* 27:8).

When Sarah told Avraham to expel Hagar the second time, it was a challenge for Avraham and was numbered as one of his ten tests. It, too, conforms perfectly to our definition of a test. He found it enormously painful. Hashem spoke to him using the same word, *b'kolah*, that Rivkah used when speaking to Yaakov:

> And the thing was very evil in the eyes of Avraham concerning his son. And G-d said to Avraham, "Do not be displeased concerning the child and concerning your maidservant. Everything that Sarah tells you to do, listen *b'kolah* (to her voice)."
>
> (*Bereishis* 21:11–12)

The word *b'kolah*, which actually means "in her voice," is an unusual usage. It should rather say *l'kolah*, "to her voice." Hashem must therefore have been conveying something more than the need to simply listen to Sarah's advice. Rashi reveals what this was in his comment on the unusual usage: *This teaches us that Avraham was inferior to Sarah in prophecy.* We learn that "*b'kolah*" means that she was prophesying!

Strangely, Rashi does not repeat his comment when Rivkah tells her son to listen "in" her voice, but the Ohr Hachaim does (*Bereishis* 27:8):

> "Listen in my voice" means that even if there is an element of deception in my voice, you should still listen. Apart from Yaakov's obligation to honor his parents, she [Rivkah] was also a prophetess, and the Torah commands us to obey the prophets' instructions (*Devarim* 18:15).

Hashem told Rivkah to do something that went against her nature. She would have to assert Hashem's perspective and desires over her own. In obeying her, Yaakov would have to do the same.

Yaakov's entire life was an expression of truth and honesty. He would keep all of the Torah's commandments even while his father-in-law was swindling him. So now, Yaakov being told to deceive his father was a real challenge for him. Rivkah's test, then, provided one for her son Yaakov as well.

Yitzchak was well aware of his son Esav's nature. He had concentrated his efforts on equipping Esav to overcome it and take his rightful place. His wife now forced him to confront the fact that all his efforts had been a failure.

Rivkah's approach meant that Yaakov received the blessings in accordance with Hashem's will. It also gave all three—Yitzchak, Rivkah, and Yaakov—an opportunity to face a challenge and discover something within themselves that they may not have thought was there. Rivkah would defy her husband only at the behest of Hashem. Yaakov would accept that truth is what Hashem says it is—and that is the only measure of truth. Yitzchak would concede that a lifetime's work and effort to mold a son had not succeeded.

This turn of events began with the selection of a wife who was the perfect match for her husband, creating a marriage with its own unique dynamic. Had Yitzchak married a woman with a temperament like Sarah's, the events that unfolded would not have produced the desired ending.

A wife has to know which approach will best guide her husband's path, whether it is the Sarah approach or the Rivkah approach. It may even be a mixture of the two. A woman's wisdom lies in matching the approach to the circumstances.

CHAPTER SEVEN

Lady Amélie Jakobovits

R ABBI DR. LORD Immanuel Jakobovits served as Chief Rabbi of the UK and British Commonwealth, which encompasses no fewer than fifty-four member states, including Canada, Australia, and India, from 1967 until 1991. He was the author of several books and a world-renowned authority on medical ethics. He was admired and respected by the Queen of England, prime ministers, and presidents. He held strong views about issues he was convinced were right and debated with Israeli politicians, *roshei yeshivah*, *gedolim*, and Israel's chief rabbis.

Immanuel Jakobovits was born in Konigsberg in East Prussia, where his father was a *rav*. The family moved to Berlin in the 1920s, when his father became a *dayan*. They moved again in 1938, fleeing Germany to escape the Nazis, and managed to reach England. Lord Jakobovits learned at London's Eitz Chaim Yeshivah and received *semichah* from three *gedolei Yisrael*: Rav Elya Lopian, Rav Leib Gurwicz, and Rav Nachman Shlomo Greenspan.

I could easily go on, expanding and adding to his list of achievements, but suffice it to say that by any measure he was a brilliant and impressive figure who was respected in both the Jewish and secular worlds. But as impressed (and even a little intimidated) as people often were when meeting the Chief Rabbi for the first time, they were equally impressed, and often more so, when meeting his *rebbetzin*.

Amélie Munk was born in Ansbach, Germany, in 1928. As the Nazis tightened their grip on Germany, her father, Rabbi Elie Munk, accepted a position in Paris as the *rav* of the Adas Yere'im Synagogue on Rue Cadet. And so, in 1936, when she was eight years old, Amélie moved to France.

The threat of Nazi Germany cast a dark and ominous shadow over France. That darkness only increased until war was eventually declared in 1939, and Rabbi Munk was conscripted into the French Army. The Germans invaded, and in six short weeks, France fell to their blitzkrieg tactics.

Over one million Parisians fled their capital as the Germans approached. Soon, Nazi troops of the 30th Infantry Division were parading triumphantly and mockingly under the Arc de Triomphe. Those who remained in Paris watched while crying in shame and trying to absorb the totality of their defeat and humiliation.

Their government had fled to the south of France, to the town of Vichy, four days before. It decided to surrender and negotiate an armistice with the Germans. When Adolf Hitler received word that the Vichy government wished to negotiate an armistice, he chose Compiègne Forest as the site for the negotiations, the place where Germany had been forced to sign the 1918 armistice after its defeat in the First World War. The signing even took place in the same railway carriage where the Germans had signed the 1918 armistice. France's humiliation was complete, indeed.

On June 22, the French Republic ceased to exist, and a puppet government controlled by the Germans collaborated with the Nazis in hunting and rounding up Jews.

Before the Germans began bombing Paris, about a million people fled Paris, among them twelve-year-old Amélie Munk with her mother and three siblings. They managed to escape on the last train leaving the city before the bombs started to fall. As she later described that journey, "The mass of people on that train, a tornado of humanity, repeatedly wrenched us from one another." It would not be the last time the family was separated.

Many years later, sitting in my house in Manchester, she spoke to some of my university students, who had squeezed themselves in to hear her lecture. There were so many people there that they resembled the passengers on that train. Lady Jakobovits told them the rest of her story of escape from the hands of the Nazis.

The train was supposed to take them to Spain—to safety. When it stopped at a station whose sign read "Albi," Amélie's mother remembered that the last letter she received from her husband was from the military base in that very town. The family disembarked, and soon, they were reunited.

In the town of Albi, the French rallied around their fellow countrymen and women fleeing the war, and for a while, the Munk family was safe. But as the months passed, the grip of the Nazis and their French collaborators tightened, and soon, Jews in France were being hunted and sent to concentration camps. When the family's situation was threatened in one place, they would join other Jews and move on to another. Amélie and her three siblings fled with their mother to Marseilles and then Nice.

In Nice, Mrs. Munk gave birth to twins, Max and Miriam. The south of France was under the control of the Germans' Italian allies, but in 1943, the Italian dictator Mussolini capitulated, and the Germans took direct control of all of France. Although they were fascists like the Germans, the Italians had not been enthusiastic about rounding up Jews, and so many had been able to survive under their rule—either hidden or openly. Now, the situation changed dramatically.

One night, there was a knock at the door of the house where the Munk family were staying. Outside stood German soldiers, and they arrested Rabbi Munk and his daughters, Ruth and Amélie. They joined 800 Jews who were to be sent to their deaths.

By a miracle, the sisters were released, and later, inexplicably, so was their father. They realized it was time to flee from France once and for all, and the family decided to head for nearby Switzerland.

The French Resistance were contacted and promised to help the Munks cross the fortified frontier. Two burly men, known as *passeurs* (smugglers), met the terrified Jewish family at night and took them to a barbed-wire fence where they had made a gap. At gunpoint, they then robbed the Munks of everything they possessed and told them to climb through the space the smugglers had made. As soon as they were through, they assured them, they would be in Switzerland and free.

The Munks crawled through the gap and arrived at the bottom of a steep incline only to find that they had come upon a river. This was something the gallant French Resistance *passeurs* had omitted to tell them. They decided to wait for morning before crossing, since they were, after all, now safely in neutral Switzerland.

At that point, baby Max started to cry loudly and uncontrollably. Nothing his parents could do would stop his cries. Suddenly, the little group was bathed in the beam of a flashlight. A Swiss border guard had heard the baby's cries. He had just had a baby himself, and his sympathy was aroused. He helped the family cross into Switzerland, explaining that where they were, huddled by that river, they had not been in Switzerland at all. In about an hour, the Germans would have arrived on their nightly patrol to pick them up and send them to their deaths.

The day that Amélie and her family were saved was Erev Rosh Hashanah, 1943.

When the war was over, the Munk family made their way back to Rue Cadet. Amélie was then seventeen, and she was not the same person who had fled Paris five years before. Her experiences of the Holocaust had, of course, affected her as well as everyone she loved. They made her feel that her only justification for being chosen to be one of the living was to help the rest of the Jewish people who had survived. As she put it, "I have to justify to myself in some small way for having survived the Holocaust by giving of myself to others, to those who have less. Otherwise, there would be no reason for me to be alive."

Her sister recalled an incident that demonstrated that Amélie's decision to give of herself to others started immediately after they returned to France. Many concentration camp survivors, she related, made their way back to Paris. Amélie was very involved in helping them. A couple with a baby were living nearby. The child tragically died, and Amélie became totally involved in helping them, giving them all the physical and emotional support she could. When the baby passed away, she performed the mitzvah of *shemirah*, staying many hours through the night to watch over the deceased child.

Lady J. concluded her talk by lightening the mood. She told the story of the first time she and her husband went to stay with the Queen of England at Windsor Castle. Her face lit up with delight as she explained how she had headed to the famous Marks & Spencer department store to buy a new set of outfits for the occasion. When they arrived at the castle, married couples were each assigned their own separate bedroom connected to each other by a shared bathroom. This arrangement was necessary, since each guest was assigned his or her own butler or maid who would attend to their every need.

After dinner (where a special kosher meal had been prepared at the highest standards for the Queen's Jewish guests), Lady J. schmoozed with the Queen and the Queen Mother (the Chief Rabbi was schmoozing with Prince Philip and Prince Charles), delighting them by telling them that her husband proposed to her at the top of the Eiffel Tower. Finally, the Chief Rabbi and his wife retired for the evening and went up to their rooms. When she entered her room, she discovered that her maid had unpacked all her belongings and carefully put them in drawers. The maid had also left her nightgown beautifully folded at the foot of her bed. Her husband entered his own room to find that his butler had done the same with his belongings, but had taken out Rabbi Jakobovits's *tallis* and laid it beautifully at the foot of his bed just as the maid had done for Lady Amélie's night attire. The butler had assumed that this unusual garment, the likes of which he had never seen before, was what Orthodox Jews wore in bed!

The students and everyone listening burst into laughter.

I had watched Lady Jakobovits as we entered my dining room where she would speak. One could sense something tangible and unmistakable as she sat down and smiled at all those young faces. She exuded a presence that drew them to her like iron filings to a magnet. It reminded me of the charisma that *Chazal* say Naomi had, which was in fact why she was called Naomi. It was the name others gave her. Everyone perceived something special, unique, and good about her. Everyone loved her, especially her daughter-in-law, Rus. It was precisely that feeling that filled the room the moment Lady J. arrived. Everyone loved her, too.

By the time she finished, she had totally captivated her audience. More importantly, she had inspired them.

Lady J. often recalled her emotions when she met the Queen for the first time. She told people she had been overcome with feelings of awe and gratitude to Hashem that someone who had literally been hunted as a child was now being welcomed by royalty.

I don't think I ever met someone whose *chessed* was quite like that of Lady Jakobovits. It seemed to me to be simply supernatural. This trait aligned perfectly with another remarkable aspect of her personality: People found it impossible to refuse anything she asked of them. That combination meant that she was able to support a large number of *tzedakah* causes. After she passed away, her children found that she was associated with over fifty charities, including Yad Sarah, Jewish Care, and Chai Cancer Care.

I had firsthand experience with her special brand of kindness. When Lady J. heard that my late wife was ill, she made it her business to get to know her and called her from London to see how she was doing. From that phone call, an instant friendship grew, and Lady J. visited our home to give a talk to my students and encouragement to my wife. Other visits and countless other calls followed. The effect of her friendship on my wife's morale (and mine, too) was incalculable.

When I was still learning at Gateshead, one of my *rabbanim* gave me a stern warning: "Stay away from Rabbi Jakobovits!" I was perplexed, and he elaborated on his warning, explaining that he would try to recruit me as a rabbi for one of the many synagogues that he represented.

Many years later, when I was learning at Liverpool Kollel, I gave a *shiur* in my home to around thirty ladies. My wife opened the dining room door to tell me I had a phone call. I was very surprised to be interrupted. My late wife would never disturb a *shiur* I was giving. I gave her a quizzical look, and she said, "It's the Chief Rabbi!" My audience was immediately impressed, and I excused myself to take the call.

The prediction of my *rav* from Gateshead some years before had proven prophetic. Lord Jakobovits wanted me to become *rav* of one of his shuls.

I was, of course, aware that the Chief Rabbi was paying me a compliment, but I wasn't really keen on taking this path for my career, and I managed to avoid his invitation. It was a good thing that he didn't have his wife call me. As I mentioned before, no one was able to say no to Lady J., and my life would have turned out to be very different.

Many years later, the phone rang at a sad time in my life, and once more, it was Rebbetzin Jakobovits. My late wife had passed away after a five-year battle with cancer, and I had just gotten up from the *shivah*.

It was the week before Shavuos, and Lady J. had made a decision. She decided to send me and my three unmarried children to spend Yom Tov in a kosher hotel in Switzerland. I liked this idea even less than the thought of being the rabbi of a shul. Still raw from my loss, I told her clearly and ungallantly that I simply wouldn't think of it. Lady J. told me she fully understood and didn't make the slightest effort to change my mind. I don't know if I congratulated myself that I had actually managed to do what hardly anyone else had by refusing this great lady. If I did, it would have been premature: She already had another plan in place.

I started getting phone calls from friends in London telling me that they had heard about Lady J.'s wonderful idea, and how they thought it would be a good thing. Then, Rebbetzin Ehrentreu (another great lady it's hard to say no to) called to add her voice. After that, Lady J. called again "just to see how I was doing." In the course of the call, she somehow managed to mention that two of my dearest friends, Dovid Rosenberg and Alan Goldberg, had put together the money needed for that idea of hers.

"I don't know if you remember it," she casually mentioned. "It was the one about you and the children going away for Shavuos?"

It was no good. I gave in, and we went to Switzerland.

Of course, Lady J. was right. It was precisely what we needed at that time. I have always been enormously grateful to her for that *chessed* to my family.

I discovered that we were not the only ones to receive calls, visits, and good ideas from Lady J. In fact, I was genuinely surprised to learn that almost everyone I knew who was struggling with a serious illness somehow had inexplicably received a phone call or a visit from this astonishing woman. I still can't figure out how she heard who was ill and what their condition was, but she did and immediately acted to lift them up.

Her relationship with her husband, though, provided me with my biggest surprise in getting to know this remarkable woman at least a little. Her daughter, Esther Pearlman, reported a truly amazing thing about her parents:

"My parents had a fantastic marriage. They were the total opposite of each other, as opposite as you could possibly get. That taught us how opposites can really complement each other.

"They loved each other deeply, and they completely respected and supported each other. You need different people in life to be able to complement each other. My father was a very quiet and extremely shy person. He was also very strong-minded and controlled, doing things very much according to plan. My mother was spontaneous, open, friendly, and bursting with *joie de vivre.*

"Despite or maybe because of their differences, they created a fantastic environment to grow up in—because we saw everything. We had the whole gamut of human emotions within one household. We learned this just by being there and observing it all."

Lady J.'s ability to create such a successful marriage and home was not an accident or the product of good luck. She thought long and hard about how to create that home and consequently was able to pass on her approach to others. She often told other women, "The goal is not perfection but harmony."

I well recall her looking sternly at me when she asked me a question about my children. When I replied, I referred to them as "my children." Lady J. shook her head at me and said forcefully, "It's not 'my children.' It's '*our* children.' Your wife's children and yours!"

Sometime after my late wife's passing, I remarried and took my new wife to meet the person I knew would instantly perform her "magic" and do for her what she did for everyone: turn her into a friend and make her feel welcomed and special. I was not disappointed.

During that visit, I noticed the famous "list" that people had told me about that was fixed to Lady J.'s fridge. It was her ten commandments for a successful marriage:

1. Respect.
2. Patience.
3. Tolerance.
4. Trust.
5. A spouse takes priority.
6. Sharing.
7. Love.
8. Giving.
9. Praising.
10. Saying "sorry."

"My mother always supported my father," her daughter Esther Pearlman related, "making him the front man even though she would make quite a lot of the decisions. She would always defer to him and make him the leader. She absolutely lived for him. She would tell us and everybody else that your first priority in life is your husband. 'If you make him king,' she would say, 'you will be treated like a queen.'"

We wrote in the chapter about Rivkah Imeinu that everyone knows that all marriages are made in Heaven, but people often forget that all marriages are made *differently* in Heaven. The formula that makes a marriage work is unique to every couple. But remembering those ten ingredients in Lady J.'s "recipe," I think that all of those ingredients have to be present in every marriage, even if the balance of the ingredients might have to be altered and tweaked.

I don't believe for one moment that Lady J. considered herself in "awe" of her husband in the same way that Rivkah Imeinu was in awe of her husband or that she didn't believe herself worthy of him. I am equally convinced, in fact more so, that Rabbi Jakobovits would have found that notion laughable. But number five on her list does show that there was more than a little of Rivkah's attitude toward her husband in Lady J.'s attitude toward hers.

Lady Jakobovits was often referred to as the "first lady of Anglo Jewry" or sometimes the "Queen Mother of British Jews." That was quite an accolade for a woman who, a few decades before, had been a girl hunted by the Nazis.

CHAPTER EIGHT

Leah: Ruchniyus without Limits

THE STORIES CONTAINED in the Chumash often seem puzzling and incomplete when read without the guidance and insight of *Chazal*. The simple reason is that they are. Without the explanations of the Gemara, Midrash, *Zohar*, and other teachings of *Chazal*, they are a locked door that lets you know that something lies on the other side but won't open so that you can see what that something is.

If we are deprived of those teachers, those *keys*, the events of Leah's life, seem very sad, indeed. She was the elder of two sisters (some opinions say they were twins). The younger was extraordinarily beautiful, while she was not. She knew that it was likely that she would be married to someone she desperately did not want to marry and instead ended up the wife of someone who desperately did not mean to marry her. It would appear that her husband hated her and could not rid himself of the conviction that the outcome of her deception was that their children, and certainly their first child, were flawed as a result of her deceit.

The real story of Leah, once we turn to *Chazal* to open the door, is remarkably different. It is one that offers inspiration and awe that such a Jewish *neshamah* existed. It offers an invitation to any Jew, man or woman, to try to emulate her.

We first meet her in *Parshas Vayeitzei*:

> Lavan had two daughters. The name of the elder was Leah, and the name of the younger was Rachel. And Leah's eyes were tender, and Rachel was beautiful in form and beautiful in appearance.
>
> (*Bereishis* 29:16–17)

Rashi explains that Leah's tender eyes were caused by her constant tears:

> She thought she was fated to marry Esav, and so, she cried. Everyone said, "Rivkah has two sons, and Lavan has two daughters. The older [daughter] for the older [son], and the younger [daughter] will marry the younger [son]."

The Midrash comments that included in "everyone" was the angel who calls out, before any person begins to be formed in their mother's womb, "This girl will marry this boy" (*Midrash Rabbah, Bereishis* 70:13).

"Everyone" was right about Leah's *shidduch*. It had been settled in Heaven years before. She *was* fated to marry Esav. This raises the obvious question: If that's the case, then why was she so resistant to marrying him?

The image that the name Esav conjures up in most people's minds would obviously provide an immediate and straightforward answer to that question. He was the portrait of a murderer, the father of Rome, where gladiators were forced to fight to the death. He was the quintessential anti-Semite whose hatred of Jews and Jewishness is eternal: *Esav hates Yaakov* (*Sifri Bereishis* 33:4).

Once more, though, we have to look at the situation through the eyes of *Chazal*, and when we do so, a far more complex picture emerges. Rav Dessler explains, based on his understanding of *Chazal*:

> This much is very clear: Esav was not predestined to be a *rasha*. Even if we find many indicators that show he had a nature that was predisposed to evil…these only point to the

kind of battles he would have to wage. Through exercising his free will, he would have been able to overcome all of those predispositions and would have triumphed by following the path his father laid out for him.

(Michtav Me'Eliyahu, vol. 2, p. 205)

Furthermore, in *Devarim*, we find that Rashi clearly dismisses the superficial and one-dimensional view so many have of Esav.

Devarim is where Moshe points out all the mistakes that Klal Yisrael made during their forty-year journey to the border of Eretz Yisrael. But he waits until the end of the journey and the end of his life to do so. Rashi explains why:

Moshe rebuked them only a short while before his death. From whom did he learn that this was the right thing to do? From Yaakov, who rebuked his sons only a short while before his own death. He said, "Reuven, my son, I will tell you why I did not rebuke you until now. It was in case you would abandon me and join my brother, Esav!"

(Rashi, Devarim 1:3)

How could anyone imagine that Yaakov Avinu's firstborn son, the founder of one of Klal Yisrael's *shevatim*, would forsake his father and join the man who represented the prototype Nazi and who rejected everything his father stood for?

The answer is simple: The caricature is wrong.

In *Parshas Beha'aloscha*, we learn that Aharon carried out Moshe's instructions on how to light the Menorah perfectly. Rashi states, *This tells you the greatness of Aharon—that he didn't alter Moshe's instructions* (*Beha'aloscha* 8:3).

This is puzzling. Surely the fact that Aharon was one of only three individuals in history who died by the "kiss" of Hashem would reveal something of Aharon's greatness, as would him being the peacemaker of the Jewish people. His unquestioning acceptance of the death of his two sons and his happiness at his younger brother superseding him also eclipse the simple fact that he lit the Menorah exactly as he was instructed.

Rav Simcha Zissel Ziv of Kelm points to another truly amazing midrash:

> It is written, *God saw the light that it was good* (*Bereishis* 1:4). Hashem said, "I do not know which of the two is better: the deeds of righteous or the deeds of the wicked." When the Torah states, *God saw the light that it was good*, it is telling us that Hashem concluded that the deeds of the righteous are better.
>
> (*Bereishis Rabbah* 3:8)

Rav Simcha Zissel explains that the wicked also want to perform mitzvos, but only great and lofty deeds like saving someone's life and other such dramatic acts (*Ohr Rashaz* 497). But tzaddikim do not ascribe greater value to one of Hashem's mitzvos over another.

Esav was like that. I once saw in a *chassidishe sefer* that when Esav asked his father, "How do you *ma'aser* straw? How do you *ma'aser* salt?" he was displaying his profound interest to do precisely the kinds of mitzvos to which Rav Simcha Zissel is referring: the great and lofty deeds.

To *ma'aser* food is to elevate it. Straw, the most basic of all foods, is food for cattle. Salt is the king of all foods. It preserves food, extending its life and bringing out the flavor of other food. Esav was using these two foods as a metaphor for human beings, the spiritually lowest and the spiritually highest. When Esav asked Yitzchak how to tithe these foods, he wanted to know how to take those on the lowest spiritual level and bring them higher—*kiruv rechokim*. He also wanted to know how to take those already on the highest levels, perhaps those attending the most elite yeshivos and *kollelim* in the world, and create a "super *kollel*" with them, elevating Torah study to yet unheard-of heights. And not only did Esav want to know how to do it, he wanted to *do* it!

Of course, that is not the Torah's approach. As the Mishnah states, *Be as particular with an easy mitzvah as with a challenging one* (*Avos* 2:1). This was epitomized by Aharon, who valued the mitzvah of kindling the Menorah as much as any other mitzvah—an approach that Esav definitively lacked.

But it's not hard to imagine that with the guidance of a good wife, and certainly a great one, this incorrect approach could be adjusted to become the correct one. There is hardly any doubt that Leah could have fulfilled precisely that role. After all, Yaakov was punished later for preventing Dinah from doing that very thing when he returned to Eretz Yisrael and Esav came out to confront him. As the Torah states:

> He arose during that night, and he took his two wives and his two maidservants and his eleven children, and he crossed the ford of Yabbok.
>
> (Bereishis 32:23)

Rashi comments:

> But where was Dinah? Yaakov hid her in a box and locked her in so that Esav would not lay eyes on her. As a consequence, Yaakov was punished for denying her to his brother, for perhaps she could have caused him to improve his ways.

If Dinah "perhaps" could have done this, Leah certainly could have. We know this from evidence supplied by Esav himself.

After Yaakov followed Rivkah's instructions and took the blessings from his father, his parents sent him away to flee from his brother's anger and to find his own *zivug*:

> Esav saw that Yitzchak had blessed Yaakov and sent him to Padan Aram to take from there a wife when he blessed him and he commanded him, saying, "You shall not take a wife from among the Canaanite women."
>
> (Bereishis 28:6)

The Alshich emphasizes that Esav understood both parts of his father's instructions: Take a wife from the family of Lavan, and do not take a wife from among the Canaanites. Three *pesukim* later, the Torah tells us that Esav emulated Yaakov by following half of his father's instructions. He did not marry a Canaanite woman—instead, he married a daughter of Yishmael.

As Rashi points out, *Everyone said, "Rivkah has two sons, and Lavan has two daughters. The eldest son will marry the eldest daughter, and the youngest son will marry the youngest daughter.*" Esav knew this. He knew that the option was available to him, but he feared and rejected it. He was afraid that Leah would change him.

If that is so, if Leah had the ability to turn Esav around and that was meant to be her mission in life, then Leah's behavior is all the more perplexing. Why did she shed so many tears? Why did she fight so hard to change her fate?

The question is especially vexing when we consider the words of the *Chovos Halevavos*:

> As one who trusts in Hashem, you are happy with whatever circumstances Hashem creates for you. This applies even if the circumstances run counter to your instincts and perspective. Hashem brings challenges that are, ultimately, always for your good. It is like a mother who has compassion on her baby, washing it, diapering it, and swaddling it, even though the baby dislikes the process and struggles against it.
>
> (*Chovos Halevavos*, Introduction to *Shaar Habitachon*)

That is a perspective that I have witnessed among Jews many times. In Manchester, England, I knew a great tzaddik. He was a Satmar chassid who was universally respected among all of Manchester's many *talmidei chachamim* and was considered their peer and equal. As a boy of thirteen, he was in Auschwitz. One day, the inhabitants of his barracks were ordered to march to the gas chambers. The men were made to strip their clothes, and seconds later they stood in the concrete room awaiting the Zyklon B that would kill them.

Another Satmar chassid standing beside him asked, "Do you think that Hashem can save us even now?"

He replied, "Just as it occurred in Egypt, Hashem's salvation can come in the blink of an eye."

At that moment, the door to the gas chamber opened. An SS man had a task to be done which required very tall Jews, and a few of the prisoners, including the tzaddik whom I knew from Manchester, were plucked from the jaws of death to do the task.

My late wife's cousin, Devorah "Dora" Roberts, was one of the bravest women I ever met. She received her first diagnosis of cancer when she was still a young woman. She fought it and won. Four years later, she was diagnosed with a second, unrelated cancer. Unbelievably, another two unrelated cancers, skin and bone, attacked her. But she didn't let her situation defeat her, and she fought back with courage and determination. It helped that she had a simple and unwavering *bitachon* in Hashem, and the words, "*Gam zu l'tovah—*This, too, is for the good," were never far from her mind or her lips.

This allowed her to maintain her *simchas hachaim*, her joy in life, through every one of her illnesses, which she expressed through an amazing sense of humor. She delighted in confounding her doctors, who were pessimistic about her chances. Devorah enjoyed explaining that she was a "medical phenomenon," with professors surrounded by scores of junior doctors coming to see the woman who launched one campaign against cancer followed by another and another and, despite the chilling statistics, won.

Devorah eventually passed away when she was seventy-six years old…of a heart attack. It was *twenty years* after her first diagnosis of cancer, not the four years the doctors had predicted. Five separate cancers could not defeat or dishearten her. She understood that this was the life Hashem chose for her even though she didn't understand why. Naturally, it was not the life she would have chosen for herself, but she embraced all the pain and suffering with smiles and confidence, knowing that *gam zu l'tovah.* This, too, is for the good.

Leah Imeinu obviously had complete and absolute *bitachon* in Hashem. She certainly knew that whatever life He chose for her was only for the good. Why, then, the tears?

We will discover the real Leah Imeinu, and why she chose the course she did, more fully in the next chapter of her story. Meanwhile, there is one thing the Alshich says about her that will inspire any Jew, male or female. I should add that from what we have previously learned, it is a lesson that women will probably find easier to take to heart and put into practice than men:

From its account about Leah's tears, our holy Torah is teaching us the vital message of how much a soul can gain when it petitions

Hashem and pleads before Him. To put it simply, through that pleading, all the greatest forces in the universe directing their most powerful efforts against you will not win.

Let us consider Leah's situation. Rachel was preordained to be the wife of Yaakov and not her. Her pleas and tears changed all that, though there were four irresistible forces gathered against her:

1. It was preordained that Rachel would be the perfect match for Yaakov.

2. Rachel, not Leah, possessed outstanding beauty.

3. Yaakov loved Rachel, not Leah.

4. Yaakov had meticulously and exhaustively designed events to make sure that he would marry Rachel and not Leah. He specified that he would work seven years for "Rachel." To guard against Lavan's substituting some other woman who was also called Rachel, he clarified his statement and added, "your daughter." He even considered that Lavan might swap his daughters' names, so that Leah would now be called Rachel, and so Yaakov added, "your *younger* daughter." All this was in addition to the fact that Rachel was indeed decreed his *bashert* by Heaven.

Yet all these precautions did not help him achieve the result he sought. As Dovid Hamelech wrote, *Hashem is close to all who call to Him, to all who truly call to Him* (*Tehillim* 145:18). Having Hashem on her side, as those many tears of Leah caused Him to be, meant that the map of Heaven and history was torn up and rewritten. Yaakov's most careful precautions would fail, and Leah would become his wife (*Alshich, Bereishis* 29:16).

In the following chapter, we will discover why that altered version of history was the right one, after all.

Leah: Ruchniyus without Limits II

R AV DESSLER OFFERS an insight into Leah's actions in
his essay on *Parshas Noach*:

Every soul that comes to this world does so to fulfill his
or her unique role in making a *kiddush Hashem*, and it is
equipped with every single tool and resource it will need to
carry out that task. Those resources include the other half
of their soul—their husband or wife. The Gemara says that
those resources are even announced by Heaven at the moment of conception (*Sotah* 2b). The announcement includes
which house they will live in and what "field" they will own—
that is, whether they will be rich or poor. The Gemara adds
that the tools include a person's physical robustness, intel-
lectual prowess, and other qualities (*Niddah* 16b).

All of these are essential to equip the soul for the role it
has to play. This is in fact the meaning of a person's *mazal*.
It refers to a soul's mission and how it is equipped to carry
it out.

The term "tzaddik" defines someone who doesn't use any of the tools he or she was given for their own enjoyment or pleasure at all. They "hand those tools back," so to speak, at the end of their journey for inspection, knowing that they will show that they were used exclusively for the mission of *kiddush Hashem.* Not one second was wasted or stolen for the tzaddik.

The Gemara states that Rabbi Yehudah Hanasi was one of the richest men in human history (*Kesubos* 104a). On his deathbed, he famously raised his hands to Heaven and declared, "Ribono Shel Olam, You know that I toiled in the study of Torah with all my ten fingers, and I did not derive any benefit from the world even with my little finger!"

There is, though, another possible role that a soul may attain for itself after it arrives in this world. That is to change its *mazal,* enlarging it beyond its original parameters [either negatively or positively]. In doing so, it will also, perforce, change the tools and equipment that it was originally assigned.

If a person succeeds in doing this, he will receive his own reward in Heaven plus the additional rewards that have lain unclaimed by those who failed to carry out their mission. Avraham, for example, claimed his own reward as well as the reward of the ten generations who squandered their own chances in this world. His *mazal* was to be the father of a place called Aram, but he extended his role to become the father of all the nations and carried out all of the roles they rejected.

Now, we can see the distinction between a tzaddik and a *chassid.* If someone fulfills his role perfectly, he is a tzaddik. There are, however, levels beyond fulfilling one's role that changes his *mazal* as he embraces the role of *chassid* and seeks to broaden the mission he was sent here to perform.

(*Michtav Me'Eliyahu,* vol. 2, p. 158)

So changing your *mazal* is possible, and that was exactly what Leah sought to achieve, moving from the role of Esav's wife to that of the wife of Yaakov.

Rav Dessler addresses this idea further in an essay entitled "*Rachel v'Leah*":

> Yaakov served Lavan for seven years for only one purpose: to marry Rachel. But there were two stages and evolutions of Yaakov's life. One was called "Yaakov," and the other was called "Yisrael." These two names and the lives they define are different levels of attachment to Hashem...Rachel and Leah were perfectly matched to Yaakov, but only at one of the two levels. Rachel was the perfect match for Yaakov. Leah was the perfect match for Yisrael.
>
> (*Michtav Me'Eliyahu*, vol. 2, p. 218)

The Shem Mi'Shmuel takes us even deeper into understanding the intensity of Leah's tears and her struggle against Heaven's decree that she should marry Esav. He points out that there were two well-known trees in Gan Eden. One was the tree of life and the other the tree of knowledge of good and evil. Both were there for the exact same purpose: to perfect Adam. Each offered a different approach. Those two approaches were personified in Yaakov and Esav. As we saw earlier from Rav Dessler, Esav's approach offered a path to perfection no less than that of Yaakov. As Rav Dessler put it, Esav was not *fated* to be bad:

> This much is very clear: Esav was not predestined to be a *rasha*. Even if we find many indicators that show he had a nature that was predisposed to evil...these only point to the kind of battles he would have to wage against them.
>
> (*Michtav Me'Eliyahu*, vol. 2, p. 205)

Dovid Hamelech famously wrote, *Run from evil and do good* (*Tehillim* 34:15). Yaakov's role was "*aseh tov*"—to do good. As such, he sat in seclusion from the world in the tents of Shem and Ever, learning Torah and fulfilling his spiritual role.

Esav's mission was different. He was meant to engage with the world, rejecting its evil and fleeing from it. That was the role for which his father, Yitzchak, had groomed him. But Yitzchak didn't recognize that his son Esav, the master trapper and hunter, was as a consequence also a master of disguise and camouflage. Yitzchak didn't realize that instead of fleeing from evil, he had embraced it.

But if Esav's father didn't see through Esav's disguise, his mother did. Rivkah saw clearly that her son had abandoned the "*sur meira*" approach.

But both trees existed in Gan Eden and served the same purpose. Both approaches could lead to the highest heights, and in fact, Esav's approach could even bring someone to much greater heights than Yaakov's!

On this subject, the Shem Mi'Shmuel (*Vayeitzei*, page 356) cites his great *rebbi*, the Kotzker Rebbe, who says that there are spiritual levels which are so incredibly lofty that they are almost impossible to achieve through the performance of mitzvos and good deeds. They are, though, achievable through the rejection of evil and fleeing to the opposite extreme.

If Esav had abandoned this approach, Rivkah knew that it could not be lost from the world, and someone else would have to take it up instead. That someone would be her son Yaakov, who would now have to master both approaches: the role of "Yaakov," of doing good, and now that of the alternative approach that his brother had betrayed, that of fleeing evil, the role of "Yisrael."

This is why Yaakov's life changes completely after he takes Esav's blessings. He has to run away—and it will not be the only time he will have to run. Now his life is filled with real-world conflicts and challenges, from dealing with Lavan and Esav, to Dinah's kidnapping, and much more. His days of sitting in seclusion and peace are over. Now, he will have to apply the approach of fleeing from evil. Yet during this period, he will emerge on a new and higher level, as Yisrael.

Leah, too, knew through prophecy (as the *Midrash Hagadol* explains) that Esav had abandoned the "*sur meira*" approach. But that approach was the one that she had been designed to complement and perfect as her husband's other half. She would have been perfectly content to be married to Esav had he used his abilities to achieve what he was equipped to achieve and become who he was meant to be.

Knowing that Esav had not done what he was supposed to do, and that this role had passed to Yaakov, Leah stormed the gates of Heaven with her prayers and tears to change her *mazal* and be able to marry Yaakov.

Only marriage to Yaakov would allow her to carry out her mission in this world. That marriage would allow her to enable Yaakov to become Yisrael. In fleeing from a marriage to a man who had abandoned his mission and exchanged it for evil, Leah was doing precisely what she was sent here to do: flee from evil…and do good.

CHAPTER TEN

Rebbetzin Judy Young

MY WIFE AND I first met Rebbetzin Judy Young about fifteen years ago at a Pesach retreat organized by the Gateways organization. She had come with her husband to give *shiurim*, and, as I would discover, they were Jewish educators of the highest quality who usually fulfilled that role together as a team. On this occasion, Rabbi Young was more than delighted to allow his wife to take the spotlight while he found a quiet place to open his Gemara and learn.

Though diminutive in stature, Rebbetzin Young was overflowing with enormous energy and enthusiasm for every word of the Torah she taught, whether to the girls in the school where she was the head of the *limudei kodesh* department or to the thousand or so guests whom she had joined for Pesach.

Judy Young was born Judy Lamm, the daughter of a famous rabbi in New York. Her father, Rabbi Maurice Lamm, would go on to become the *rav* of several congregations, as well as a professor at Yeshiva University's RIETS rabbinical seminary. He was also the author of a book called *The Jewish Way in Death and Mourning*, which went on to sell over 350,000 copies.

Judy's mother was the other half of an extremely successful rabbinic partnership and an innovator in her own right. Together they created an organization to educate hospices across the United States on catering to their Jewish patients' specific needs. She continues that work today as the president of the National Institute for Jewish Hospice.

In 1971, Judy, her older brother, and her younger sister moved with their parents to Los Angeles, where her father became the rabbi of the Beth Jacob Congregation of Beverly Hills. When it was time for Judy to go to seminary, there was only one choice as far as she was concerned, or, rather, one location: Eretz Yisrael. One day, while she was getting ready for Shabbos during her year there, she was fiddling with the catch on her necklace when she noticed a strange lump on her neck. A trip to the doctor revealed that she had non-Hodgkin's lymphoma. Her parents brought her straight back to California.

Doctors were found and treatment began. It went well, and eventually, the day for her final treatment arrived. Judy was about to take her last chemotherapy pill when she stopped.

Anyone who has been involved in a fight with a life-threatening disease or has supported someone in that situation knows that it can conjure dramatic and intense reactions. For some, those reactions are negative, like frustration, anger, and depression. For others, paradoxically, it can bring calmness and wisdom. It can also bring a person extremely close to Hashem.

For nineteen-year-old Judy Lamm, it had done precisely that, and as she held that pill in her hand, she hesitated. She didn't want to simply take that last pill and go back to the way she was before she became ill. Judy didn't want to lose her newfound and intense closeness to Hashem.

She decided to call her *rav* and explained her dilemma. She received an interesting reply.

"Tell Hashem that you will work for the next five years to bring twenty-five Jewish souls who have no knowledge of *Yiddishkeit* to Torah."

Thus began Judy's double mission: to help Jewish souls and to express her thanks to Hashem through doing so.

The treatments she had gone through had left her very weak, so an immediate return to her beloved Eretz Yisrael was not an option. When she was finally able to make plans to go back, it was to accept a position she had been offered by Rabbi Dovid Refson, the founder and dean of Neve Yerushalayim, a seminary for young women who had not been blessed to be born into a *frum* family.

I have known Rabbi Refson for many years. Among his many talents is an uncanny ability to assess people and judge their character. Rabbi Refson judged that Judy would make an excellent *madrichah* and teacher for the girls in his school. It would also give her the chance to keep the promise she made while holding that last pill in her hand.

A few years later, Judy thought about starting *shidduchim*, and she returned to America. She found a job teaching in a *kiruv* school while working for a *kiruv* organization that specializes in working with high-school kids. It was clear that she had concluded that helping twenty-five souls return to Torah was only a deposit in repaying the debt she felt she owed Hashem. Anyway, the more souls she touched and helped return, the more she strengthened her closeness with Him.

The national *kiruv* organization NCSY spotted the emerging gift that this young woman possessed, and she soon found herself flying around North America from Vancouver, Canada to Delaware and Seattle, organizing Shabbos retreats and adding more young souls to her mounting tally.

Someone whose goal was as clearly defined and focused as Judy Lamm's meant that anyone she met on a *shidduch* would, of course, want to help her keep the promise she made at the end of her first treatment all those years ago. Eventually, she met a young man whose family originally came from the same town as the Chafetz Chaim and had just left Lakewood's Beth Medrash Govoha to become a teacher in Baltimore's Talmudical Academy. He knew that Judy's cancer was curable, and he was entranced by someone so devoted to building a relationship with Hashem.

Soon a glass was broken under a *chuppah*, and Judy Lamm became Rebbetzin Judy Young.

Listening to Rabbi Young tell his wife's story, I couldn't help smiling. It was quite obvious that not only had Hashem heard her solemn undertaking seven years before she met her husband, but He had provided her with every possible opportunity to fulfill it.

The new couple were approached by a Syrian rabbi who had set up a school for the new immigrants who were arriving in New York from Aleppo and Damascus. He knew that these immigrants' Jewish identity, which had been secure in their ancient homeland, was anything but secure in their new one.

Jewishness in Syria meant doing things precisely the same way they had been done in Jewish families for hundreds of years. Knowledge of *why* they were doing those things was not seen as so important. In New York, it would be crucial.

The Youngs started the "double act" that would see Rebbetzin Young multiply her original twenty-five Jewish souls to thousands.

She started a twelve-week course for the high-school seniors called "The Jewish Woman," which introduced them to the fundamentals of Jewish marriage laws and customs. The results were revolutionary. The girls found the ideas they were learning beautiful and attractive. They started repeating them to their mothers when they went home. Soon, the young *rebbetzin* found that their mothers were coming to school, too, to join her classes. They wanted to hear these beautiful ideas for themselves.

With their wives and daughters committed to *shemiras hamitzvos* and building their homes on the foundation of halachah, the men had no choice but to follow in their footsteps. Today, forty years later, the Syrian community in New York is a perfect example of the renaissance of Sephardi Torah scholarship and a source of pride throughout the Torah world. I was shown letters from some of the girls who had attended those groundbreaking classes. They included pictures of their own children's weddings and Judy's other "students"—the girls' beaming mothers (now grandmothers). Each letter attested to the Youngs' contribution to the remarkable Syrian renaissance.

In 1984, Rebbetzin Young saw a new opportunity to expand her commitment to Hashem. Yeshiva University of Los Angeles (YULA) was looking for a teacher for their boys' school, and Rabbi Young fit the bill perfectly. Both husband and wife were on their radar.

As her family grew, Rebbetzin Young had a rule that whenever they moved to a new city, she would stay at home for the first year to concentrate on her children and make sure that they had settled well into their new lives. But since she only had one small child when she arrived in LA, she was able to throw herself immediately into her new teaching position, adding to her "score" in her connection with Hashem.

Teaching at the girls' branch of YULA was an obvious first step in their new lives in LA. Then it occurred to Judy that if "The Jewish Woman" course had been so effective with the Syrians in New York, perhaps it would appeal to the Californians in Los Angeles.

It did, and the numbers attending the course meant that it would be repeated many times.

Four years later, another invitation came the couple's way as their reputation as educators kept growing. This one came from the city of Palo Alto in Silicon Valley, about an hour from San Francisco. The small Orthodox Jewish community was struggling to establish a school for their children, and they needed a rabbi and *rebbetzin* who could build one. They also needed to appoint a rabbi and *rebbetzin* for their shul. The Youngs filled both requirements perfectly.

After two years of building a school and a community, the number of people looking to "steal" the Youngs for their own community increased. The much larger *kehillah* of Atlanta, Georgia, persuaded them to move south. So the Youngs moved again, with Rabbi Young accepting the position as principal of the Torah day school there.

Rebbetzin Young stayed at home for the first year, making sure her children were settled as they embarked on the next chapter of their life. After that first year, she partnered with the local *kollel* and started once again running programs for women under the banner of the Binah Institute for Women. Once more, her passion and effervescence proved irresistible, and women arrived in droves to join in the programs and, crucially, kept coming back.

During the Youngs' second year in Atlanta, a new baby daughter arrived in the family, and after seventeen years of remission, so did the cancer.

By this time, Judy's parents had retired and moved to Palm Springs in southern California. They decided that their daughter should have her treatment once more in Los Angeles. Rabbi and Rebbetzin Lamm rented a house near the hospital, and Judy's mother looked after her, shepherding her daughter to and from treatments.

The Young family were split into two. Rebbetzin Young still wanted to fulfill her role as a mother, so three of her children came to be with her, while the rest stayed with Rabbi Young in Atlanta. The grueling treatment took its toll, and the family were reunited only twice during their six-month separation.

What did Rebbetzin Young think when the disease came back? As she told my wife, "I never thought, *Why me?* Instead, I thought, *Why not me?*"

Her husband told me that it only galvanized her to do more—to multiply her promised twenty-five Jewish souls many more times than she already had. Her closeness to Hashem was certainly not diminished in the slightest. As soon as she recovered, she saw the perfect way to increase her efforts.

A new school had been established in Queens, New York, to cater to the influx of a different kind of Sephardi Jew who was now arriving on America's shores. The year was 1993, and the great migration of Bukharan Jews from the former Soviet Union was at its peak.

The school board's requirements were perfectly matched to the ones the Youngs possessed. Once again, Hashem made it obvious that He had heard her solemn undertaking, and once again He provided her with the perfect tools to keep it. Rabbi Young became the dean of the school, and his wife served as the principal of the girls' division.

That was when my wife and I met the Youngs for the first time, when we taught together at a Gateways Pesach program. We became fast friends after that, and we would stay with the Youngs often when we visited New York. On one Motza'ei Shabbos, they told us that they were going out for their weekly "date night" and invited us to come along.

The venue for their "alone time" was a Waffle Bar restaurant on Central Avenue in Cedarhurst. The place was packed with teenagers doing what teenagers do best: making lots of very loud noise.

I cannot recall what my wife's reaction was to this "treat," but I was convinced that I was there to atone for something really bad I had done in a previous *gilgul*. Rebbetzin Young smiled at me as though we had landed in paradise and said, "Isn't this fantastic? We love it here! We so love seeing the kids having a good time."

Despite all her struggles and pain, Judy Young's devotion to young Jews wasn't diminished in the slightest.

The Bukharan school blossomed under the guidance and care of Rabbi Young and his wife, who still overflowed with enormous energy and enthusiasm for every word of the Torah she taught.

Rebbetzin Young's cancer came back a third time, and a third time she fought it off and carried on precisely as she had before. Over the next two years she even led Aish HaTorah trips to Eretz Yisrael for the summer, relishing in the participants' rambunctiousness and clamor and adding once more to the number of souls she set on the road to discovering Hashem and His Torah.

A few months after that second Aish HaTorah trip we were staying with the Youngs when my wife and I had to fly to Cincinnati, where I would be speaking that Shabbos. When I turned on my cell phone after Shabbos, there was a voicemail from Rabbi Young waiting for me. Judy had gone to sleep after attending a *sheva brachos*, where she danced with her hallmark enthusiasm on full display. She returned her *neshamah* to her Creator as she slept.

I recall a visit to my *rav*, the Gateshead Rav, Rav Betzalel Rakow. During the course of our conversation, he mentioned that someone I knew and respected in the community had passed away. I was quite shocked and immediately asked, "How old was he?"

The *rav* raised his eyebrows at me and replied, "How old was he? He was precisely the age when Hashem Yisbarach wanted his *neshamah* back again."

Judy Young beat cancer three times and was at precisely the age when Hashem Yisbarach wanted her *neshamah* back again. When He did, He brought home a woman who had an insatiable appetite to bring Hakadosh Baruch Hu as many *neshamos* as she possibly could and show her *hakaras hatov* for allowing her to come so close to Him.

CHAPTER ELEVEN

Rachel: Others above Self

I N LEARNING HOW Leah was ultimately meant to be Yaakov's wife, we learned much about Rachel. There is, though, much more still to discover.

The Midrash points to the *pasuk* that reports that at the end of his life, Yaakov *bowed down at the head of the bed* (*Bereishis* 47:31) and comments:

> Rabbi Chanina says in the name of Rabbi Shmuel, the son of Rabbi Yitzchak: Upon discovering Leah's deceit, Yaakov wanted to divorce her. When he saw that Hashem had sent him so many sons through her, he thought again. In the end, he accepted and understood the correctness of her actions. Who was "the head of the bed" to whom our father Yaakov bowed? It was Leah!
>
> (*Midrash Rabbah, Bereishis* 71:2)

The Eitz Yosef elaborates on the words of the Midrash, explaining that Yaakov asked Yosef to make sure that he was buried alongside his fathers in the Cave of Machpeilah because he wanted to be buried alongside Leah. By now he was quite certain that she was truly meant to be his wife, and that even in death they should be together.

Yaakov saw that Leah had given him six sons and a daughter. From those sons would descend Klal Yisrael's *levi'im* and *kohanim*. From those sons came Dovid Hamelech and the line of Mashiach. And he realized that he could not have fulfilled his mission without her. Yet the Midrash points to another *pasuk*, the one that informs us that *Rachel was* akarah *(barren)* (*Bereishis* 29:31), and seems to give an explanation that contradicts the one above:

> Rabbi Yitzchak says: Rachel was the *ikarah*, the "main part" of Yaakov's house... Rabbi Shimon bar Yochai learns that since everything [concerning the creation of Klal Yisrael and the *shevatim*] came about through Rachel; therefore, all of Klal Yisrael are known as her children. That is why the *pasuk* states, *So says Hashem: "A voice is heard in Heaven... Rachel crying for her children..."* (*Yirmiyahu* 31:14).

Rachel, who was buried by the road where the Jewish people would pass on their way to exile, would cry for all of them, and they would stop to cry to her to petition Heaven for them. Even those who were not directly descended from her were nevertheless called her children. This fact was recognized by every individual in Klal Yisrael then, and it is still recognized now.

The *Navi* informs us that when Boaz married Rus:

> All the people who were at the gate of the city and the elders who were witnesses said, "May Hashem make the woman who is entering your house like Rachel and like Leah, both of whom built up the house of Yisrael."
>
> (*Rus* 4:11)

The Midrash observes:

> The people should have mentioned Leah first, stating "like Leah and Rachel." Yet despite the fact that Boaz and all the members of the Sanhedrin were descendants of Leah, they recognized and knew that the *ikar*, the heart of Yaakov's family, was Rachel, for Yaakov only served in Lavan's house for her.
>
> (*Yalkut Shimoni, Rus* 606)

It might be useful at this point to recall the different roles the two sisters filled. Leah was the ideal partner when Yaakov took on the additional role his brother Esav rejected. Now he would look outward and engage with the world. Rachel was the perfect match for Yaakov before that new role began, when he was the man who disengaged from the world and looked inward, focusing on self-improvement and perfection. That was precisely Rachel's focus, too.

There are two discordant notes that Yaakov strikes and verbalizes in his relationship with Rachel, and we will visit both of them in this chapter.

The first is when she turns to her husband in desperation and says, *Give me children, and if not, I am dead* (*Bereishis* 30:1). This same *pasuk* informs us that *Rachel saw that she had not borne [a child] to Yaakov, and Rachel envied her sister.*

Let's pause to allow Rashi to explain what the Torah means by "envied":

> Rachel was jealous of Leah's good deeds. She said, "If she had not been more righteous than me, she would not have merited children."

Though often touted as a negative trait, jealousy can be used positively, as *Chazal* teach, *Jealousy between* talmidei chachamim *leads to an increase of Torah knowledge* (*Avos* 4:21). When *talmidei chachamim* see others who are greater than they are, they consequently strive to be greater and know more Torah. Envy becomes the vehicle for the amount of Torah being learned to be expanded. (Rav Yosef Salant, in his *sefer Be'er Yosef*, famously counsels against this approach, pointing out that jealousy used in this way can too easily be subverted by the Satan to become the other kind of jealousy—*his* kind, the source of *sinas chinam*.)

The Torah continues:

> She said to Yaakov, "Give me children, and if not, I am dead." Yaakov was angry with Rachel and replied, "Am I in the place of Hashem, who has withheld children from you?"

The Alshich explains what Rachel meant when she said that if she didn't have children, she was "dead":

> I fear that my jealousy of my sister will be corrupted, growing into rivalry and hatred. I will be considered as "dead" even while I live if I have become infected with the sin of *sinas chinam*.

Rashi says here that Rachel was asking Yaakov to *daven* for her, as his father had *davened* for his mother, Rivkah. Her pleading was met by a seemingly callous and heartless reply:

> You ask me to be like my father, but I am not like my father. My father had no sons when Rivkah begged him to pray for her. I have sons. The problem lies with you, not with me.

It's hard to imagine such a lack of sympathy and kindness from an ordinary husband toward his wife. In Yaakov's case, it's simply impossible to imagine. But through the careful analysis of *Chazal*, we don't have to.

Before examining their words, I must pause to tell you a story that I first wrote about in my translation and commentary of *Sha'ar Habitachon* from the *Chovos Halevavos*.

When my wife and I moved to America, it was to accept a job offer that was promised to last three years. The promise evaporated after only ten months. This left us in a financial crisis with a mortgage to be paid for our house back in England and the rent for our apartment in Brooklyn, along with all our other bills, of course.

I sought the counsel and advice of my great *rebbi*, Rav Matisyahu Salomon *shlit"a*, whom I have known for over forty years. I began by explaining our situation. Then I explained that even more than the financial crisis in which we found ourselves, I was worried by my reaction to it.

I said, "Rebbi, you have known me since I was a very young man in Gateshead Yeshivah. I think I am a *ma'amin* and a *ba'al bitachon*. But if that's the case, then why am I *so* worried?"

I concluded by saying, "I feel like a complete fraud."

Rav Matisyahu looked at me and replied, "Maybe you are a fraud!"

You might think it was a harsh comment, but I didn't. I wanted an answer to why I was so worried. I welcomed those words and the challenge they presented to me. Perhaps I *was* a fraud or, if not a complete fraud, someone who was comfortable ignoring the fact that I had much more work to do on the project that I was solely responsible for—the project called "Yehudah Yonah Rubinstein."

I should add that Rav Matisyahu had lots of help and suggestions to offer, as well as love and affection for an old *talmid*. But here is a good piece of advice from me to you: Do not seek the view of a *litvishe mashgiach* who has a *yekeshe* background unless you want to hear the truth. I did, and knowing me for so long, he knew that I did. He knew that he could tell me what the truth was, even if it left me feeling uncomfortable. (It was actually this crisis that led me to publish this new translation and commentary of *Sha'ar Habitachon*, the classic work on *emunah* and *bitachon*, which I called *Refuas Halev*.)

The Alshich explains what was really behind Yaakov's apparent harshness to his wife. Rachel was actually concerned that Yaakov bore some resentment against her for choreographing the deception that led to him marrying Leah. This is why she asked him to *daven* to Hashem. That would let Heaven know that Yaakov held no grudge on that account, and the blessing that had been withheld from her could now be given.

Yaakov explained to her that in fact he held no grudge. Through his marriage to Leah that Rachel had engineered, he had been given sons. She sought a solution through him for a problem that did not exist. Rachel had to look elsewhere to find the cause and the answer.

Rachel had to look within herself, and indeed, as Rashi explained, she recognized the possibility that she could have done more in self-improvement and good deeds. She immediately acted and, for a second time, offered to take a painful path in order to benefit another. It was the same path she had taken before, and now, she allowed another woman, Bilhah, to marry her husband. Through that kindness, any deficiency in her heavenly account might be paid up.

Rachel's path, after all, was the same as Yaakov's: to look inward and strive for self-improvement and perfection. The way to do that takes us back to our earlier discussion as to why women are innately more spiritual and on a higher level than men. It is because women possess less of a sense of "I" than men do. Rachel's road to becoming the "*ikarah*," the heart of Yaakov and Klal Yisrael, was born through her determination to reduce and eventually eliminate her sense of "I."

Rav Levi Yitzchak of Berditchev explains, in his *Kedushas Levi*, the scope and depth of Rachel's first act of abandoning her "I" for the sake of another—when she acted on her sister Leah's behalf. The *pasuk* tells us, *And [Yaakov] also came to Rachel, and he also loved Rachel more than [or, rather, because of] Leah* (*Bereishis* 29:30). The *Kedushas Levi* states:

> We should ask what is the purpose of the second "also" in the verse. Light is shed on the question later when the Torah reports that Rachel gave birth to her first son, Yosef: *And God remembered Rachel* (*Bereishis* 30:22).
>
> Rashi comments what it was that Hashem "remembered": Hashem remembered that she had revealed the signs that she gave over to her sister Leah. He also recalled that she was troubled that she would fall into Esav's lot; perhaps Yaakov would now divorce her because she had no children.

The *Kedushas Levi* points out that at first it seems that Rashi is offering two separate reasons for Hashem granting Rachel a child, but in reality, both are intertwined elements of the same reason. Consider: Why would Rachel worry that Yaakov would divorce her because she didn't have children? He had no need to divorce his childless wife to find another who could give him children. He already had children from Leah, as well as from Bilhah and Zilpah.

However, in engineering that Leah would take her place and marry Yaakov, she had no guarantee that he would still want to marry her at all. That would leave her vulnerable to taking Leah's place as the wife of Esav. Yet Rachel was still willing to run that risk to save her sister.

That is why, the *Kedushas Levi* concludes, the second "also" appears in the *pasuk* quoted above. Yaakov understood Rachel's motivation. The love the Torah says he felt for her from the moment they first met was now increased and amplified "also" because of Leah—because of what Rachel had done for her sister.

This realization simply confirmed that Rachel was indeed the *ikarah*, the heart of Yaakov, someone who was working to eradicate her sense of "I," as he was. That primary mission remained unaltered, even though he took on an additional mission, picking up the role left behind by his brother.

If we return briefly to the midrash quoted above that points out that Rachel was the *akeres habayis* (*Midrash Rabbah, Bereishis* 71:2), we learn another amazing aspect of Rachel being the beating heart of Klal Yisrael: the fact that her son Yosef carried on her role and her path.

It is not only Rachel who became the parent of the entire Jewish people—Yosef did, too! That's why the *pasuk* in *Amos* (5:15) states, *Perhaps Hashem will comfort the remnant of Yosef.* Although the *pasuk* is referring to all of Klal Yisrael, they are called "Yosef's remnant."

There is another aspect to the legacy of Rachel and her son Yosef. The concept behind the role of Mashiach ben Yosef, who will arrive first to pave the way for Mashiach ben Dovid, is beyond the scope of this book. But we can say that just as Leah and her children owe their existence to Rachel, Mashiach ben Dovid, Leah's descendant, owes his existence to Rachel's descendant, Mashiach ben Yosef. It is he and only he who can challenge Esav's grip on Klal Yisrael and cause it to loosen and as a consequence cause Esav's world to come crashing down. As the prophet Ovadiah predicts, *The house of Yosef will be a flame and the house of Esav straw* (*Ovadiah* 1:18).

In his Haggadah, *Leil Shimurim*, the Aruch Hashulchan explains why Yosef will consume Esav:

> Why do we have four cups of wine at the Seder's reconstruction of the Exodus? Rabbi Yehoshua ben Levi says it is because of the four cups of wine mentioned when the wine butler related his dream to Yosef:
>
> *"And the cup of Pharaoh was in my hand, and I took the grapes and squeezed them into Pharaoh's cup, and I placed the cup on Pharaoh's palm." And Yosef said to him, "This is the meaning [of your dream]: The three vine tendrils are three days. In three days' time, Pharaoh will elevate and return you to your position, and you will place Pharaoh's cup in his hand"* (*Bereishis* 40:11–13).

The obvious question is: What does this episode have to do with Pesach and the Exodus from Egypt?

It is written, *A voice is heard in Heaven, lamentation, bitter crying, Rachel crying for her children* (Yirmiyahu 31:14). Why is only her crying heard? All the mothers of Klal Yisrael were saints.

The main cause of crying among the Jewish people was Amalek, the Babylonians, and the Romans—Esav's descendants. They destroyed our Beis Hamikdash, enabled by the *sinas chinam* that infected the Jewish people.

To state the obvious, if someone comes to lodge a complaint with the authorities against another, he or she must not be guilty of the same crime they are accusing the person of doing. It is for this reason that when the other *Imahos* cry for their children, their prayers are not as effective as Rachel's prayers. Their sons are guilty of the crime of *sinas chinam*, too, through their sale of Yosef. But Rachel and her sons, Yosef and Binyamin, were free of this stain. That is why it is her crying that is heeded in Heaven.

It is also for this reason that the first king of the Jewish people came from the tribe of Binyamin. He had to destroy Amalek, and being free of any association with his brothers' crime of *sinas chinam* against Yosef, he could pave the way for the kingship of the house of Dovid.

This brings us back to the four cups of wine that Yosef heard about in prison. The actual story was that both the baker and wine butler were jealous of each other and then grew to hate each other. Each plotted against the other, the baker putting a fly into the cup of Pharaoh and the butler putting a stone into the dough that would be made into a loaf for Pharaoh's table. Each hoped to cause the other's downfall.

Since it was almost certain that Pharaoh would drink the fly but not so certain that he would bite on the stone, the baker was executed, but the butler was forgiven.

The message to Yosef was that all exiles and the

destruction of both Batei Mikdash would be caused by *si-nas chinam*: His own exile and imprisonment was due to his brothers' jealousy. His fellow prisoners' "exile" in that Egyptian prison was due to their hatred for one another. The second Beis Hamikdash was destroyed by baseless hatred. The Gemara (*Yoma* 9b) says that the first Beis Hamikdash, too, ultimately fell due to *sinas chinam* between the great sages of the time.

(*Aruch Hashulchan, Leil Shimurim*)

Rachel followed her husband's admonition to look within herself and purge any vestige of jealousy she felt toward her sister. Yosef continued in this path: Despite his brothers' jealousy and hatred toward him, he never felt hatred toward them.

The path that Yaakov, Rachel, and Yosef all took remains the cure and solution to bringing an end to this *galus* for us today. It requires introspection, looking inward at who you are and who you want to be. That path requires you to look and see if you really are the "real deal" or if you are perhaps even a *little* bit of a fraud.

Focusing on improving yourself means you meet others who may have more possessions, talent, or even Torah knowledge than you without becoming jealous, which is the soil from which hatred grows. It allows you to become part of the *antidote* to Esav. You will be the antithesis of the man who exchanged greatness for opprobrium. He allowed his engagement with the world to turn *sur meira v'aseh tov* into *mekabel ra v'aseh ra*.

So, we see that Rachel's path will pave the way to the completion of the process. That completion will be through Leah and Dovid's descendant Mashiach and the building of the third and final Beis Hamikdash.

There is still one unanswered question we have to answer about Yaakov and Rachel. The Torah reports that after the seven years he worked to marry Rachel were complete, *Yaakov said to Lavan, "Give me my wife, for I have completed my days—v'avo'ah eileha"* (*Bereishis* 29:21).

I intentionally did not translate the last two words for the reason that Rashi explains:

> These words that Yaakov used, even the crudest person would not use. It was only so he could father generations [of Klal Yisrael] that he spoke this way.

Yet again, a simple and superficial understanding of Yaakov's words would still leave us feeling uncomfortable and confused.

By looking afresh through the eyes of *Chazal*, we will come to an important discovery about the journey of the *Imahos*. It will be a theme that will link many of the women in this book. To find it, we will have to properly come to know Lot's daughters—two of the greatest women in the Torah.

CHAPTER TWELVE

Mrs. Shani Lisser

GETTING ANY JEW to allow you to write about them is almost always a struggle. Jews are programmed to run from honor. If you want a Jewish woman to tell you her story, you have to take into account the quality of innate *tznius* we wrote about earlier.

When Mrs. Shani Lisser allowed me to include her story in this book, it was on the strict condition that I focus on the problems that she and others are trying to solve rather than her as a person. As those problems are ones dear to my own heart, I was happy to accede to her demand. I did explain that I would have to write a little about her, simply to put the project she is involved with into context, and she kindly agreed.

The next hurdle to overcome was finding a time to interview her. Mrs. Lisser, I discovered, is a very busy lady.

We spoke briefly by phone and arranged that I would phone her the next day, late in the morning, for a longer discussion. As I live in New York, and she lives in London, which is five hours ahead, late morning for her would be early morning for me.

I called her at six o'clock in the morning, and when I got through, she apologized and said that she was in the middle of another call and asked me to call back an hour or an hour and fifteen minutes later. I happily agreed to do so and went to *daven* Shacharis.

When I returned to my desk, I called again, but this time her phone was busy. I called a second and third time and finally left a voicemail message. Shortly afterward, my phone rang, and it was Mrs. Lisser, apologizing again. She had been on the same call for nearly two hours, helping someone who needed her expertise and advice in the area to which she has dedicated so much of her time and efforts: helping children who are going or have gone off the *derech*.

I first met Mrs. Lisser and her husband, Moshe, sixteen years ago. The friendship with Moshe was instant and has lasted to this day. My admiration for both has also remained the same. Actually, it has grown.

One of five children, Shani Sipper was born to German parents who had managed to escape Hitler. Her father arrived on one of the Kindertransports that brought children to England, while the British denied the same haven to their parents. They had to send their children to safety while staying behind as Europe's doors ominously shut. Yet Shani's mother somehow managed to arrive in the UK together with her entire family.

Shani's family settled in the Stamford Hill area of London, and Shani attended the nearby Lubavitch school. From there, she joined the famous seminary that Rav Dessler founded in Gateshead. Two years later, she became engaged to Moshe, and they soon married. Her husband was already managing the business his mother had started when she arrived in Britain after her liberation from Auschwitz. Under his direction, it grew into the internationally famous Hermolis kosher catering company.

The new couple waited four and a half long years before they were blessed with their first baby, a little girl. Moshe and Shani's joy and profound feelings of gratitude to Hashem Yisbarach brought them to a decision: They decided they were going to adopt other Jewish children.

Mrs. Lisser told me that because they were very young, their naïveté and enthusiasm prevented them from realizing at first that there were very, very few Jewish babies available for adoption, and sadly, there was a very large number of Jewish parents all competing with them to offer those babies new homes.

"It was a strange thing," she said. "I remember once, in school, when I was around eleven or twelve, a teacher asked our class what we wanted to do when we grew up. The girls all started providing the standard and normal answers you would expect. I said that I wanted to open an orphanage."

She told me she still does not have a clue what made her say that. I pressed her and asked if perhaps there was someone in her family who had adopted or fostered a child, but there was no one. Shani recalled that her father had always been involved in *chessed* and was very active in one of the UK's very first *kiruv* initiatives, the East End Jewish Scholarship Center in London. She thought that perhaps that had something to do with it.

Mrs. Lisser may not have been able to explain her unusual youthful ambition, but it would turn out in the end to not have been far off the mark.

With the plan to adopt a baby an impossibility, the Lissers carried on with building their own family. The idea of adopting lots of children ended up getting pushed aside because, as Mrs. Lisser put it, "life got in the way." But a few years later, life decided to oblige them by moving aside and getting out of the way again.

Someone called Mrs. Lisser and explained that there was an eighteen-year-old young man from the UK's other major Jewish community, Manchester. He had run away from home and had nowhere to go. Could the Lissers have him to stay "just over Yom Tov"?

They could. The young man ended up stayed in his new home, with his new "parents," for two years. Indeed, the Lissers did become the boy's new mother and father, eventually arranging his *shidduch* and making his wedding. They still serve as his mom and dad and, actually, his children's grandparents, too.

As their family grew and more of their own children arrived, so did other teenagers who had left families who could not cope with them or they with their parents. Instead of becoming lost to the Jewish people, they found a safe place and a new family where they were welcome and felt a sense of belonging.

Moshe told me that although he fully supported his wife's

"orphanage," he left her to run it while he ran his business. "It was Shani's project," he said simply.

Fostering a young man who has suffered emotional abuse, sometimes of the most terrible kind, is unsurprisingly not an easy task (my late wife and I fostered precisely such a young man). The task of undoing years of terrible damage is simply enormous. One of the teenage boys who became part of the Lisser family had suffered physical abuse at home, eventually repaying it in kind and leaving his home for good. One night, one of her husband's business associates was visiting the Lisser house and witnessed a scene that appalled him.

The Lissers' latest foster son, though only fifteen and below the legal age to get a driving license in the UK, had been sneaking out at night and stealing Shani's car. It was always returned before the Lissers awoke, and they would never have found out, but suddenly, Mrs. Lisser noticed that her mail was full of tickets for having illegally parked her car in places she had never been. The truth came out on the night the business associate was visiting, and he observed the scene unfold from the hallway below.

As she stood talking to the boy, she told him that his punishment would be that he would have to hand over his cellphone and lose the use of it for a day. The young man's temper, formed by the abuse he had suffered at home, erupted, and he stepped menacingly toward his new parent. She knew that in the past, when he had behaved this way toward his parents, it had resulted in him assaulting them. But though his body language declared that history was about to repeat itself, he managed to pull back and handed over his phone.

The guest later told his hostess, "When he moved toward you, I was convinced he was going to hit you…and you didn't even flinch."

Mrs. Lisser calmly explained that she didn't flinch because she knew that he would not lay a finger on her. "They hand over their hearts when they join our family," she said. "I knew I was quite safe."

The more teenagers passed through the Lissers' doors, the more the Lissers grew in experience and understanding the causes that brought these kids there.

Soon, an appalling pattern emerged. With only one exception, all of the teenagers had suffered molestation and abuse before they arrived.

Almost always, their parents had known nothing about it. They simply could not understand why their child was an erupting volcano, with devastating results for them and all the other members of their family. All they knew was that they could not handle their child anymore, and he would have to leave home.

When I spoke to Mrs. Lisser, it was shortly after her youngest daughter had gotten married. She no longer fosters children, and her "orphanage" has closed its doors. The reason is that Mrs. Lisser's now vast experience has led her to the conclusion that there is a much better way to deal with this issue than provide a place that can become a teenager's new home. She can help the families they come from deal with their children's pain so that they don't have to leave.

This was why Mrs. Lisser couldn't speak to me when I called at the arranged time to interview her. She was busy advising a parent how to handle an angry teenager who resembles a volcano ready to erupt and stop it from erupting at all. It was a call that lasted nearly two hours. Problems like these demand as much from a person that they can possibly give to solve the pain and despair that can push young Jews to the edge—or over it.

Mrs. Lisser found a remarkable young rabbi who is also aware of the problem of children in danger of leaving their homes and Hashem behind. Together, they have set up an organization called Unconditional Parenting. Shani Lisser counsels parents in techniques on how to help their children. Her associate, Rabbi Schwartz, deals with the kids themselves and their relationship with their schools.

That brings me to the end of telling you a little of Mrs. Lisser's story or, more precisely, stories. I hope I have kept my part of our agreement and focused on the desperately needed work she and her husband have done as opposed to who she and her husband are. I hope, though, she will forgive me if I repeat what I said at the beginning.

I have known Mrs. Lisser and her husband for sixteen years. My admiration for both has also remained the same.

Actually, it has grown.

CHAPTER THIRTEEN

Lot's Daughters: Tzidkaniyos Misunderstood

IN CHAPTER TWO, we saw how the female line of Avraham's house was spiritually stronger than that of the males, and we explained why. This point is perfectly illustrated by Lot's daughters.

Lot, like Sarah, was the child of Haran, Avraham's brother. That made him Avraham's nephew and brother-in-law. He was also Avraham's *talmid*.

The ambivalence Lot's father showed toward Avraham's faith and his family's belief in Hashem was echoed in his son. At first glance, it seemed to be echoed, too, in Lot's daughters. They survived the destruction of Sedom along with him, but they then went on to behave, as some commentators state, like true daughters of Sedom.

Rav Dessler explains the nature of Lot's ambivalence. On the one hand, he seemed to possess much of the greatness of his uncle. On the other hand, he also had all the characteristics against which Avraham had fought all his life. What determined the man he would become?

> We see that the true merit and level of a person is not determined by the mitzvos and good deeds he does, because he was educated and trained in those. His spiritual

status is determined solely by the level he has achieved as a consequence of his choices. The Torah education he received merely determines the point at which he will begin to exercise his own choices in areas in which he has not been educated.

(*Michtav Me'Eliyahu*, vol. 1, p. 115)

Rav Nosson Tzvi Finkel explains that Avraham had mastered the *middah* of *chessed*, kindness, to such an extent that he personified and exemplified it. Simply by coming into contact with him, one's own sensitivity and practice of *chessed* became elevated to the point of willingness to be sacrificed for it. Lot was one of those who became "infected" by Avraham's *chessed*. When two strangers appeared in Sedom, he passionately begged them to accept his hospitality. When they accepted, he went to extreme measures to protect them from an attack. All this confirmed the level of his attachment to *chessed*.

As Rav Dessler states elsewhere, this incident came after the death of his *other* daughter (*Michtav Me'Eliyahu*, vol. 2, p. 167). She, too, had offered hospitality to a stranger, which was a capital crime in Sedom, and she was tried and sentenced to death. Her punishment could not have been crueler: She was eaten alive by insects. Lot was made to witness it, and yet when the opportunity to repeat her *chessed* offered itself immediately afterward, he did not hesitate.

So we are faced with a mystery. After this incident, when the Heavenly decree to destroy Sedom was issued, *Hashem remembered Avraham and sent Lot from among the destruction* (Bereishis 19:29). Rashi explains what it was that Hashem remembered about Avraham that caused Him to save Lot: *He knew that Lot was aware that Avraham had told the Egyptians that Sarah was his sister, and he didn't reveal the truth.* This is astonishing. Lot was a man whose greatness in *chessed* reached the point of self-sacrifice and death. Would that not have been reason enough to save him from Sedom's destruction? Yet it was the fact that he did not betray his uncle, brother-in-law, and *rebbi* to Pharaoh, which would have resulted in his death, that was the cause of his life being spared.

From this, we can clearly see that the level a person reaches as a consequence of *chinuch*, of training and education, even if he reaches the pinnacle of that level, does not define the *real* person. When and how he defeats his own negative nature does.

Lot's negative nature becomes apparent when we ask an obvious question: What was such a *ba'al chessed* doing living in a city where *chessed* was a crime punishable by death?

The answer is revealed in the reason for the split between the *rebbi* and his *talmid*: money.

Avraham's shepherds saw Lot's shepherds grazing on other people's land. As *talmidim* of Avraham, they rebuked the shepherds of Lot, and that started a fight. Avraham didn't want the conflict to spread to him and his nephew, so he proposed that each go their own way. Lot chose to settle in Sedom, because he saw that it was an extremely rich land and he would consequently have plentiful grazing for his cattle and flocks. In simple language, Lot could get rich in Sedom, and Lot loved money and was motivated by wealth.

Had Lot given in to his base nature and betrayed Avraham, he would have brought about his teacher's death. Sarah would have been taken by Pharaoh as a wife, and Lot would have become the brother-in-law of the richest man in the world. That was a test, indeed, for someone whose prime focus was money.

We can now reconcile what seems to be a contradiction. The real Lot was not a true *ba'al chessed*. The real Lot was a materialist. In denying his basic nature and rejecting his *yetzer hara's* suggestion that he betray Avraham and as a consequence have access to unimaginable wealth, he merited being saved from Sedom.

As we have learned, the female line is spiritually superior. Now we can understand properly what appears to be the shocking behavior of Lot's daughters after their escape from Sedom. The Torah informs us:

> And Lot went up from Tzo'ar and stayed on the mountain with his two daughters, for he was afraid to stay in Tzo'ar, and he and his two daughters lived in a cave. The elder daughter said to the younger, "Our father is old, and there is no man left alive on earth to marry us, as would be the normal custom of all the world. Let us go and give our father wine to

drink and lie with him and bring to life seed from our father."

And they gave their father wine to drink on that night, and the elder one came and lay with her father, and he did not know of her coming or going. And it was in the morning that the elder daughter said to the younger one, "I lay with my father last night. Let us give him wine tonight, too, and you go and lie with him and give life to his seed." And they gave him wine on that night too, and the younger one lay with him, and he did not know of her coming or going.

Lot's two daughters conceived from their father. The elder daughter gave birth to a son, and she called him Moav; he is the father of [the nation of] Moav until this day. The younger also bore a son, and she called him Ben Ami; he is the father of the children of Ammon until this day.

(*Bereishis* 19:30-38)

The Midrash points to the words that the eldest daughter chose to say: *Bring to life seed from our father* instead of *Bring to life a son from our father* (*Midrash Rabbah, Bereishis* 51:8).

In his commentary on the Midrash, the Eitz Yosef says that the "seed" referred to is the seed of Mashiach. The word for seed, *zera*, is related to the word *zar*, meaning strange or foreign. This intimates that the seed of Mashiach will emerge from a "strange" and unexpected place—from Moav, who was conceived in a union between Lot and his daughter, and from the unexpected union of Yehudah and Tamar.

Another hint to this is in the name Moav itself: *mem, vav, aleph,* and *beis.* When these letters are spelled out in full (מ"ם ואו אלף בית), they have the same numerical value as the words *mimenu yotzi haMashiach*—"from him will come the Mashiach."

As the Midrash says, the daughters believed that the entire world had been destroyed just as it had been destroyed by the Flood in the time of Noach (*Bereishis Rabbah* 51:8). The evidence before their eyes easily justified that conclusion. The mighty cities of Sedom, five in all, were reduced to rubble—with no survivors. They didn't have any way to call or contact anyone to see if any others in the world had survived. They assumed that they were the sole living beings left alive. This led Lot's eldest daughter to conclude that the only way that humanity could continue was through them, the only survivors, the three people in that cave. She was, in fact, convinced that this was Hashem's will.

The Alshich echoes the words of the Midrash, saying that their intention was solely for the purpose of continuing mankind and bringing the Mashiach. Lot's motivation, though, was far from being so pure. It turns out that he did know what had happened the first night but still allowed himself to be plied with drink so that it could be repeated on the second.

There is therefore ample evidence revealed through a careful reading of the Torah's description of the incident, as well as the words of *Chazal*, which attests to the sincerity of Lot's daughters. There is additional support that comes from a more surprising and recent source. We glimpse it in a story that was once told by the *gadol hador* and tzaddik Rav Moshe Feinstein.

It happened in the year 1922, in Lyuban, Belarus, where Rav Moshe was serving as rabbi. Rav Moshe was summoned to the bedside of a member of his *kehillah*, a man who had become very ill. When he arrived, the man explained that he knew why he had been afflicted with this illness.

At the Shabbos table that week, the man had discussed the week's *parshah*, *Vayeira*, and commented on the behavior of Lot's daughters after the destruction of Sedom. He was harsh and scathing in his criticism of what they had done with their father.

That night, two very old ladies appeared to him in a dream. Their dress conformed to the strictest laws of *tznius*, and they told the man that they were Lot's daughters. They had heard his harsh criticism of what they did and had come from Heaven to reveal their motives to him. They explained that after Sedom's destruction, they had believed that everyone in the world had perished. The only way for humanity to begin again was through the only three remaining survivors: Lot and his daughters.

They could have pointed out their familial connection to the tzaddik whom the entire world recognized and respected—Avraham Avinu. They could have hidden their actions and claimed that they had become pregnant through some "miracle." They could have even founded a religion that would serve as a precursor to the one that would make precisely such a claim about its origins two thousand years later.

However, to make sure no such claim was possible, they called their children by names that made it clear that every human child has a father of flesh and blood. For this reason, they called their children "Ben Ami" (Ammon), meaning "the son of my nation," and "Moav," meaning "from my father." In the merit of exposing themselves to criticism and shame for the glory of Heaven, in the merit of their honesty, the authentic Mashiach would emerge—the very opposite of a false messiah, who would emerge from a lie.

They concluded that this man who had become ill had sinned very gravely by speaking about them as he had. His punishment was to be measure for measure and would resemble that of the spies who disparaged Eretz Yisrael: Their tongues were twisted, which led to their deaths.

After the Jew concluded his story to Rav Moshe, he turned his head to the wall and died.

CHAPTER FOURTEEN

"Debbie"

MANY MODERN-DAY OBSERVERS of the Torah world have taken to using the phrase the "post-*kiruv* age" to describe our time. During the sixties and seventies, there was a flood of college-age young men and women who came in throngs to yeshivos and seminaries to discover Torah and make *shemiras hamitzvos* their life. In the following decades, the flood slowed until it was a steadily flowing stream. Today, the stream of Jewish college-age kids who attend yeshivos and seminaries is going against the current and has been reduced to a trickle.

In 2005, the Novominsker Rebbe *zt"l* went to London to honor the UK's Project SEED as it celebrated twenty-five years of success in the field of *kiruv rechokim*. At the end of his address, he paused, changed direction, and grew pensive. "Today," he said, "we are witnessing a new phenomenon. It is something that we have not witnessed before: children in large numbers going off the *derech*.

"That," he concluded, "has to become our new focus."

Around that time, I was invited to deliver a keynote speech to the Association of Jewish Outreach Professionals at a huge annual gathering of *kiruv* professionals. The topic I chose posed a question: "Helping Them Going Up, Helping Them Going Up, Catching Them

Falling Down: How Appropriate Is the *Kiruv* Professional in *Kiruv Kerovim*?"

Many of the most successful figures in the field of *kiruv rechokim* made that same journey themselves. They are obviously best equipped to guide others in traveling the path they once took. Indeed, they are admired and respected for going on to become *rabbanim* and *rebbetzins*, with some distinguished *talmidei chachamim* among them. They can share their experiences and struggles with their *talmidim* and *talmidos*. They've *been* there.

It is a very different story in the world of *kiruv kerovim*. The road of a *ba'al teshuvah* who started from a nonreligious home is a totally different journey from that of a *ba'al teshuvah* who came from a house where mitzvos were kept.

For a man to stand up in front of a Jewish audience to tell his story of rejection and journey away from the Torah is to ask a lot. To ask a woman who has returned to admit that there was a time when the Torah's most fundamental laws and values, like Shabbos and *tznius*, were disregarded and her world resembled that of Orpah more than that of Rus, is to ask the impossible.

I was recently speaking at a Shabbaton. After I finished, a *frum* lady approached me. She began to tell me her story, and then, she burst into tears.

Debbie was born into a *frum* New York family. Tragically, it was a very unhappy one. Her parents both came from families of Holocaust survivors. Those experiences left them stern and emotionally cold. Their four children never heard the words "I love you." They never received a hug.

There were also constant fights between the mother and father, which had a terrible effect on the children. At the age of nineteen, Debbie followed in the footsteps of her older brother, who had already left behind the battleground masquerading as a home.

The Alshich wonders why two brothers, Machlon and Kilyon, who both married out of Klal Yisrael and left Eretz Yisrael, who were both guilty of identical crimes, suffered different fates. Machlon was given a second chance, and his soul returned to this world as Rus's son Oved. Kilyon was given no further chances.

The Alshich answers that Kilyon married out first. This weakened Machlon's resolve, so eventually, he followed his younger brother's lead. Machlon, then, was not as guilty as his brother, and their crimes were not exactly identical, after all.

When Debbie's brother Yanky walked away from his family, he also walked away from Torah and mitzvos. Debbie followed in his footsteps, and they led her to places and people that stirred painful memories, memories that interrupted the telling of her tale, producing uncontrollable sobbing instead.

But the parallel to Machlon and Kilyon is flawed. They did not take the opportunity during their lifetimes to do *teshuvah*. Yanky and Debbie did.

Once again, Yanky made the first move. He was reasonably sure that the journey would be one that would end with a warm "welcome back." Debbie did not have the same confidence. What would people think of her? What would they say and what would they not say about the life she had led while she was gone?

Debbie's road would be a much more difficult one to travel, but two years after Yanky came home to Torah and *shemiras hamitzvos*, Debbie did too.

She had been visiting an old friend in Yerushalayim, who insisted that she come with her to visit one of the Holy City's tzaddikim, Rav Asher Freund, the founder of Yad Ezrah, which provides aid to the needy on an epic scale. Debbie resisted. She was too filled with guilt about her recent behavior. But eventually, she took the first steps that brought her home again.

Rav Freund assured her that absolutely nothing she had done was beyond Hashem's power to forgive. Intensely embarrassed by her recent history, Debbie replied that, "Hashem will laugh in my face."

The only laughter came from Rav Freund, who told the young woman firmly, "No, He won't. Hashem loves you."

Debbie found that the *rav* was right. Klal Yisrael, too, was far more willing to forget the disastrous diversion her life had taken than she had ever imagined.

Shortly after, Debbie met her *chassan*, and Hashem smiled on her return by giving her children. Her brother Yanky had already moved forward and built his own home and family, carefully constructing it to be the antithesis of the unhappy home in which he had grown up. His house was a happy place filled with laughter.

But one day, abruptly, the laughter stopped. Yanky, the father who had been so determined to build a family where smiles would be the decorations of his home, suddenly became ill. A short time afterward, he passed away.

Debbie told me that six months after her brother's *petirah*, he came to her in a dream.

His face shone with a smile as he said to her, "Tell me all your *aveiros*!"

She shook her head and said she couldn't. There were too many, and they were too awful.

Her brother's smile widened. "I *know* what they were," he said emphatically, "and I want you to know that I did all of them, too!" Debbie listened, transfixed, as he continued, "But it doesn't matter. Once you have done real *teshuvah*, as you have, they don't exist anymore."

That was when Debbie woke up. Her brother and the dream were gone, but for the first time since she took her first steps to come home, the crippling guilt of the choices she made when she had left *Yiddishkeit* was gone, too.

This may indeed be the "post-*kiruv* era," at least as far as *teshuvah* applied to the hippies who once stood at the Kosel and somehow found their way from there to a *ba'al teshuvah* yeshivah or seminary. But the era of *teshuvah* is never over.

Now the focus, though, as the Novominsker Rebbe pointed out, has to be on bringing children from *frum* families—our families—home again. It will help and encourage them to do so, whether a young man or a young woman, to repeat the words of Rav Freund: "Hashem won't laugh at you for trying. Hashem loves you."

CHAPTER FIFTEEN

Tamar: Mother of Mashiach

THE STORY OF Tamar is one of the deepest and most troubling in the entire Torah. To understand it even a little, we first have to establish certain facts about her story, as well as that of Yehudah and his sons. After we have done that, we will hopefully be able to begin to explain the dramatic climax of her story, when she is taken out to be burned to death and still refuses to publicly embarrass Yehudah by revealing that he is the father of the twins she is carrying.

The key to unlocking this series of events that are a puzzle within a riddle wrapped up inside an enigma lies in Rashi's commentary on the *pasuk* that tells us that Tamar sent Yehudah the possessions he had given her to prove that he was the father of the children she was carrying: *A Heavenly voice came forth and declared, "The entire series of events came about entirely through Me"* (*Rashi, Bereishis* 38:26). Rashi goes on to explain that since she acted modestly in Yehudah's house, Hashem had decreed that kings would be descended from her, and ultimately, so will Mashiach.

The obvious question is: Why did Hashem engineer the journey of this crucial link in the chain of events that would lead to the birth of Mashiach to come about precisely in this way?

Let's start at the beginning.

The conflict between the brothers and Yosef climaxed in their decision that he should die. Yehudah intervened and suggested that his sentence be commuted to being sold as a slave instead. When they saw the agony that Yosef's disappearance caused their father, they were smitten with remorse. They blamed Yehudah, believing that if he had done more to change their minds, they would have listened.

The story of Yehudah and Tamar therefore begins with the words, *And it was at that time that Yehudah went down from his brothers* (*Bereishis* 38:1). Rashi explains that the word "*vayeired*—and he went down" means that the brothers' accusation that he could have done more resulted in his being demoted in their estimation and status as their natural leader. This, in turn, caused him to leave them.

The Alshich points to the opening word in the story, "*vayehi*—and it was." This term always points to something bad occurring. The Alshich says that in this case, the bad thing was, *Vayehi ba'eis hahi*—"the *time itself* was bad." Rav Shlomo Wolbe explains this crucial concept:

> Anyone who has ever learned Torah over a substantial period in a yeshivah or seminary will know well that there are times of tremendous spiritual growth and other times where one finds oneself falling. These times are constantly changing, with one retreating and giving way to the other.
>
> (*Alei Shur*, vol. 1, p. 34)

This is a phenomenon that affects not only individuals but also the entire world, over the entirety of history, as Rav Dessler makes clear:

> It is not for a commemoration of past events that we celebrate our festivals. Rather, we return annually to the source of the original event and to the holiness of that moment in time, which recurs every year.
>
> (*Michtav Me'Eliyahu*, vol. 2, p. 21)

We see that there are certain times in the year, times marked by our festivals and fasts, that echo the events that they commemorate. In addition, there are unique moments in time that offer those who recognize them and seize them fully gifts that they may bring to Klal Yisrael and the world. Yehudah failed to grasp such a moment and save Yosef, and so, he fell spiritually. Eleven years later, Tamar would be told, *Your father-in-law is going up!* (*Bereishis* 38:13). She seized that moment and secured the journey of Mashiach over the generations.

Tamar was the daughter of Noach's son, the prophet Shem. But having greatness in your family is no guarantee that you will take it and utilize it to help you grow. Tamar did so, and Yehudah realized that she was worthy of marrying his sons and that Mashiach would descend from her.

But Yehudah's plan was flawed. He had married a woman whom the Torah does not name. Rav Dessler states that any individual who is named in the Torah was a great person (even if that means being great in wickedness, such as Bilam or Pharaoh). At a time when Yehudah was still spiritually wounded and recovering from his failure to save Yosef, he may have thought he was marrying someone who would be a worthy partner in ushering the next phase of Mashiach's journey, but he was wrong. The person who would do that would be his daughter-in-law.

Yehudah's wife gave him three sons. The messianic line that flowed through him merged with her line, and as a result of this mésalliance, it was diverted from its correct course.

Imagine a scientist who has been working tirelessly for decades to find the cure to cancer. He discovers an extremely rare compound, and only the tiniest amount can be produced. The good news is that only a minuscule fraction is needed for combination with other compounds to create the cure. But while marrying the compounds together with the others, a calamity occurs in the laboratory. The scientist's assistant presses the wrong button, and the entire amount of the rare compound is combined incorrectly, producing something that is useless.

After discovering the mistake and recovering from his distress, the scientist goes about remedying the disaster. He extracts the rare compound from the wrong ones and then combines it with the correct ones to get his project back on course.

This is precisely what happened in the story of Yehudah and Tamar.

Yehudah's eldest son, Er, failed to overcome the weakness he inherited from his mother and died. His brother Onan was expected to marry

Tamar in a process that is a very close copy of the halachic rite of *yibum*. This would have allowed Er's soul to return to earth and start again. Onan seemed willing to undertake the task but repeated his brother's mistake and died, too.

There was a third brother, Sheilah, who now should have married Tamar, but, as Rashi tells us, Hashem manipulated events so that it would be Yehudah, in one of the most baffling and perplexing episodes in the history of Klal Yisrael, who would fulfill that role.

The Alshich offers a surprising explanation as to why.

The process of *yibum*, as we said, is to restore a soul to the world. If Sheilah would have stepped in and done that, then he would have succeeded in restoring a soul to the world—Onan's soul. A brother can only restore one soul—the soul of the last brother who died. He would not be able to restore the soul of the first brother who passed away, Er. Yehudah, however, could bring back both souls. After all, he brought them both here in the first place.

This brings us to the way in which he did this, once more reminding ourselves that, *A Heavenly voice came forth and declared, "The entire series of events came about entirely through Me!"*

The Shach states, in his commentary on the Torah, that all the critical marriages in the path of Mashiach share a common denominator: They are shocking and scandalous. The first one is the incestuous beginnings that came about through Lot and his daughters, which resulted in the people of Moav from whom would come Rus. The next is that of Yehudah and Tamar, where at first, Yehudah believed that Tamar was a harlot. Then, there is the incident of Dovid Hamelech and Batsheva, which led to people pointing their fingers at them and saying, "Adultery!" and "*Mamzeirus*!"

These distasteful events, the Shach goes on to say, convinced the Satan that there was no need for him to concern himself trying to disrupt these unions and the children they produced. There was no way that the critical moments in the next chapter of Mashiach that was unfolding could possibly have come about through unions like these.

The same explanation applies to Yaakov's words to Lavan when the time to marry Rachel arrived after seven long years. Yaakov uses a phrase that appears base and inappropriate. Rashi says a puzzling thing about Yaakov's choice of words: *Isn't it true that even the crudest person would not use this expression? But Yaakov meant that he intended to have children* (on *Bereishis* 29:21).

The Shem Mi'Shmuel explains what Rashi means by this by citing the Arizal: Yaakov knew very well that the arrival in this world of the souls of the twelve tribes of the Jewish people would be opposed by the Satan to the nth degree. When the Satan heard Yaakov use this expression, he was convinced that the marriage to Rachel could not be the one he had to sabotage. There was no way a marriage like this could result in producing holiness or holy children.

Rav Chaim Friedlander explains this concept further:

> The Midrash says regarding the fourth *pasuk* of the Torah that Hashem "hid" the light He created during the Creation to be given to tzaddikim in the future. Rav Dessler says that the light would show exactly what Hashem's plans were, and accordingly, the Satan would see them and do everything in his power to make sure they would not come to fruition. By hiding that light, the Satan would be unable to derail the outcomes that Hashem desired.
>
> (*Sifsei Chaim, Bereishis*, p. 455)

Let's pause and consider the role of the angel called the Satan. His job is to provide alternative choices that allow us to ignore or oppose Hashem's will. *Chazal* say that the Satan has neither pleasure nor pain when we listen to him. His task is merely to make sure we are offered alternatives so that we have *bechirah*, free will. Unless you have at least two options, you have no choice. The greater you are, the more he knows he has to "up his game" to make you fail.

It might be useful to think of an angel as a spiritual robot or an algorithm. It is created to perform specific tasks. When it has fulfilled those tasks, its job is complete. It has "checked" the box.

Rav Friedlander goes on to say:

> We now understand Hashem's approach. Whenever there is a revelation where Hashem shows His hand, it

always has to be preceded by a difficult and dark period where that hand is not apparent. Were it not so and the Satan could see Hashem's intentions, he would make every effort to disrupt it... The very times that we feel as the most painful and difficult are the ones when the Satan is unable to see Hashem's plans and disrupt them. If at such times a Jew remains loyal and unquestioningly follows the Torah and its dictates, he will reach a time when he is able to perceive and understand what Hashem intended all along.

(*Sifsei Chaim*, p. 457)

When Yehudah sought a wife for his oldest son, Er, he sought someone who would be worthy of being the mother of the next link in the chain of Mashiach. We mentioned that Tamar was the daughter of the prophet Shem, who had been the one to tell Rivkah that the pregnancy that so worried her was the result of her carrying twins. He knew that one would be a *rasha* and one a tzaddik. He knew that from these two sons, two nations would be created. He even foresaw the remarkable friendship between Antoninus, Caesar of Rome, and Rabbi Yehudah Hanasi, both descendants of Esav and Yaakov respectively. This was the stock from which Tamar originated.

As we also mentioned, much happened from the time Tamar married Yehudah's eldest son until Yehudah emerged from his spiritual decline and started to rise again: Yehudah's two eldest sons died, and his third son, Sheilah, was not old enough for *yibum*. In the meantime, Tamar returned to the house of her father, Shem, and Yehudah's own wife died. Then, *It was told to Tamar, "Your father-in-law is going up to the south to shear his sheep"* (*Bereishis* 38:13). The Alshich says that the person who told her this was her father, Shem. He knew that the time of Yehudah's long exile from his previous spiritual level was over, that he was on his way back up. Tamar didn't hesitate to seize the moment, and she changed out of her widow's clothing. Then she went in her disguise to await her father-in-law at the roadside.

What happens next in the story would succeed in bringing back the souls of Yehudah's two dead sons. It would also fulfill all the conditions necessary to confound the Satan. An assignation with a woman he believed to be a harlot, something repellent to any Torah Jew, let alone one as great as Yehudah, would never bring holiness to the world, and certainly not the soul of Mashiach. The Satan was satisfied that on this occasion, his "services" were not required.

But how could Tamar possibly know that eventually Yehudah would publicly recognize that he was the father of the twins that she would conceive? As she sat by the road, how could she possibly know that Hashem would send a different angel, one that controls human passion, to force Yehudah to stop and be the one who would do *yibum* and be the father of her sons?

Regarding this, Rav Chaim Shmulevitz states:

> Tamar's expectation that Yehudah would approach her must have been forlorn, indeed. That did not stop her from doing everything within her power to try to bring about the monarchy of Dovid and Mashiach into the world. When a person is determined to achieve greatness, he doesn't calculate or hold back—he simply acts. He examines and seizes any opportunity, even one holding only the most microscopic amount of hope… But an act of greatness does not produce mediocre results.
>
> (*Sichos Mussar*, p. 72)

So, bereft of hope but determined, Tamar was rewarded, and Hashem sent an angel to compel Yehudah so that he could not refuse her, and she would conceive (*Midrash Rabbah, Bereishis* 85:10).

When Tamar's pregnancy become apparent, she was put on trial. The sentence against her was passed in *beis din*. Yehudah himself could not sit in judgment, and instead, he sat in the court observing. Who were the judges at Tamar's trial? The Midrash says she was judged in the court of Shem!

How this could be? It was Shem who told her to meet Yehudah at the crossroads in the first place!

We have seen that Shem certainly knew that Yehudah was now recovering, or perhaps had recovered, from his disastrous fall and was on his way up, and he had informed his daughter of this. It was clear to her that he was telling her to seize this moment, that she was meant to conceive twins from Yehudah, and now was the time.

Tamar realized that in order for this to come about, she would have to be clever. This led her to dress up and play the part of a harlot. As the *Zohar* teaches, she knew what the future of her actions would produce (*Vayeishev* 189):

> She was righteous and calculated with great wisdom when she acted as she did. She put herself in this position only because she knew what would result from her actions.

There is a revealing statement in the Midrash that reports that after she left Yehudah and went to the bathhouse, she told other women there not to bump against her stomach because, *I am carrying kings!* (*Bereishis Rabbah* 35:10). So she clearly knew that from her union with Yehudah, kings—specifically, Dovid and Shlomo, who were direct descendants of her son Peretz—would be produced.

This leads us to the most troubling part of the episode: the death sentence passed on her, and her refusal to reveal Yehudah's role in her pregnancy in case he would be publicly shamed.

The Torah tells us that she was sentenced to be burned, and there is much debate among *Chazal* whether this could in any way be the appropriate punishment for her alleged crime. (The Ba'al Haturim [*Bereishis* 38:25] quotes Rabbeinu Yehudah Hachassid and says that she was actually taken out to be branded on her forehead and not burned to death.) Moreover, if the path we have steered through various statements of *Chazal* and our understanding of this episode is correct, her father, Shem, who had instigated the entire incident, could have easily revealed the true story and stopped the punishment, yet he said nothing. Tamar herself said nothing even as she was about to be offered to the flames. Finally, Hashem Himself allowed the flames to lick at Tamar's feet, awaiting Yehudah to make his choice and declare, *She is right; [it is] from me.* (*Bereishis* 38:26; *Sotah* 10b)—meaning, "She is innocent. I am the father."

Rav Dessler offers a compelling explanation of why these events had to play out this way:

> Yehudah was, from the moment of his birth, the person from whom the line of Dovid Hamelech and Mashiach would

come… But to achieve this, he would first have to reach the level where he would say, "She is right; [it is] from me," and this, too, was part of his purpose in this world.

(*Michtav Me'Eliyahu*, vol. 5, p. 175)

Mashiach will require the entire world to recognize and admit their mistakes. That same ability had to be imprinted in his very being and DNA. That is why Yehudah had to go through this process: He had to come to a point where he would have to confess to a terrible mistake.

Before Yehudah made his famous confession, this essential quality was only a potential one within him. He would need an opportunity to turn the potential into reality. Until Yehudah turned what he *could be* into what *he was*, he could not create the house of Dovid and Mashiach. He would have to embrace his potential and choose to turn it into reality, and that could only come about through the story of Tamar. He would be compelled to fall to a level where he would go to a harlot and then publicly admit what he had done, even if it was embarrassing and shameful.

The episode of Tamar and Yehudah would be imprinted in the soul of Yehudah, that of his descendants, and eventually that of his ultimate descendant, Mashiach. That quality will allow Mashiach to demand the same response from the nations of the world. And that could happen only if Yehudah was given the opportunity to be placed in circumstances where he could bequeath what he had achieved to all his future generations.

Throughout this episode, Tamar's greatness is clear. She knew that this path was essential, that it was the only path that would lead Yehudah to his confession and ultimately to the creation of Mashiach, so she acted in the way the *gedolim* of Klal Yisrael always do when Hashem demands it: They are willing to go against their nature to obey His command.

Avraham, the *ba'al chessed* par excellence, was prepared to act against his nature to take his son—his only son—Yitzchak and sacrifice him to Hashem. Yaakov, the man of truth, was willing to act against his nature to deceive his father and "steal" his brother's blessings, because Hashem told him through his mother to do so. In the future, Rus, who had rejected the infamous immorality of her people to become a Jew, would listen to Naomi and go and lie at the feet of Boaz, just as any typical Moabitess might have done.

Then there was Tamar. Rav Yerucham Levovitz tells us just how extraordinary her sacrifice truly was:

> The *pasuk* says, *And Yehudah saw her and thought that she was a harlot, because she covered her face* (Bereishis 38:15). *Chazal* explain that "she covered her face" means that she had covered her face while she was in her father-in-law's house because she was such a *tzanua*.
>
> Yehudah had never seen Tamar, and therefore did not recognize who she was when he saw her by the roadside. Now this paradigm of modesty was determined to accept the shame of sitting by the roadside, where everyone could see her, solely for a holy purpose. This was appallingly bitter and painful to such a woman and in itself was more painful than being thrown into a furnace.
>
> Tamar was willing to bear all this embarrassment to bring Mashiach into the world.
>
> *(Da'as Torah)*

Tamar, who was the *tzanua* par excellence, who was so modest, would be willing to act against every fiber of her being to adopt the appearance of a harlot in plain sight of everyone. She was willing to endure being diminished and demeaned and humiliated to allow greatness to emerge.

CHAPTER SIXTEEN

Mrs. Gigi Weiss

I OFTEN SAY IN my *shiurim* and writings that there is no such thing as an ordinary Jew. Start to ask a Jew questions about his or her life, and invariably, you find yourself hearing about events and choices that describe a life that is anything but ordinary.

That idea is expressed by Rav Simcha Zissel Ziv of Kelm, an idea we quoted earlier:

> The wicked also want to do mitzvos! But only if they are the big and extraordinary ones, like saving someone's life. That is not the perspective of a tzaddik. Avraham Avinu was visited by what he thought were three Arabs and did not know that they were actually angels. He was a hundred years old and recovering from his *bris milah*, but he and his wife ran to prepare them a meal fit for a king. He involved his then only son, Yishmael, in the mitzvah in order to teach him how to do *hachnasas orchim*... Tzaddikim expend as much effort on what appears to be a small and easy mitzvah as they would on a big and dramatic one.
>
> *(Ohr Rashaz, Parshas Beha'aloscha)*

Sometimes, though, you have to look very carefully to realize that the various small and easy mitzvos that fill an ordinary life add up to something truly great.

Tova Gittel Grosskopf was born in Manchester, England, the year after the Second World War ended, in 1946. She had two brothers and an older sister. One of her cousins found it difficult to pronounce "Gita," so Gita became "Gigi," and that name stuck with her for life.

Her parents were a "mixed marriage." Her father, Yosef Tzvi, was born in England, but his father, Gita's grandfather, came from the Ukrainian town of Brod, so his roots were set deep in the rich soil of Belz *chassidus*. Her mother, Esther, was born in the German city of Konigsberg.

Manchester, situated in the county of Lancashire, was the heart of the British textile industry, and many of the city's Jewish businesses un-surprisingly were "cut from the same cloth." Yosef Tzvi worked along-side his brother in their family business. Each of the brothers was in charge of a specific aspect of what was known as the "rag trade," supply-ing cloth to make suits for men and dresses and skirts for ladies.

The Grosskopfs became very close friends with their neighbors, Mr. and Mrs. Weiss. They even used to rent a holiday home together at the nearby seaside town of St. Anne's on Sea. That was when Gigi first got to know her future husband, Sholom. He was six and she was three, and they built sandcastles together on the beach.

Today, Manchester is an enormous Jewish center, complete with yeshivos and girls' seminaries catering to its exploding community of *chareidi* Jews. But that abundance of institutions was very far off in the 1950s. During that era when Gigi and Sholom were growing up, Gigi went to Prestwich Jewish Day School and Sholom to Broughton Primary. When she left elementary school, Gigi's next move was to at-tend Stand Grammar School for girls. It was a non-Jewish school, since there was no equivalent Jewish girls' high school at the time.

Sholom's high school career also took him to a non-Jewish estab-lishment: Salford Grammar School. When he returned home after his first day, his father asked him how it had gone. This was Sholom's first experience with the non-Jewish world, and he replied sheepishly that it had gone "okay." His father smiled and told him that he wasn't going back. A new Jewish school had opened up, and was struggling to fill its classes with boys. Sholom started his second day of high school in a very different school from his first.

It took the new Manchester Jewish Grammar School a number of years to attract sufficient numbers that allowed them to "stream" boys according to ability. In its early days, some of the boys were already familiar with learning Gemara, while some were just learning to read Hebrew. Three of the older boys were sent to spend some of their day at Manchester Yeshivah, where they would be taught at their level, returning to school for secular subjects in the afternoon.

It was there that Sholom met Rabbi Dubov, a Lubavitcher chassid who had suffered both under the Russian czar and the communists. His warmth was a magnet to many boys that drew them to the world of *chassidus*. Rabbi Dubov saw something special in young Sholom. He learned with him privately, which sealed the bond that would take him from a *yekeshe* upbringing (Sholom's father was born in Galicia, but he was brought up in a German orphanage) to a chassidic one.

Meanwhile, Gigi left high school and went on to earn a degree in education. One of her friends asked her to come and help at a forthcoming Lubavitch girls' camp, which started her on her own journey into the world of Chabad.

Sholom had by then left yeshivah and started working in his father's business. At the same time, he became very involved in Lubavitch outreach activities, and it was at one of these events that one of the *rabbanim* had a great idea for a *shidduch*. He arranged for Sholom to visit his home when the young lady he had in mind for him would also be there. At one point in the evening, he invited Sholom into the parlor to be introduced to Gigi Grosskopf. The rabbi made the formal introductions, and Gigi and Sholom burst into laughter. The *shadchan* was perplexed, and they had to explain that they had known each other all through their childhoods and used to make sandcastles together.

Soon, the young couple was married, and the new Mrs. Weiss started teaching in a local *chareidi* girls' school. The first child in what would be a large family arrived, and Gigi had to learn to juggle childrearing with her teaching.

One day, when she was walking one of her babies in a stroller, she met a friend who was doing the same with her little boy. They had an idea. Why not watch each other's babies on alternate days? This way, each would get a day off, a chance to relax and get some badly needed sleep.

The idea worked like a dream, and soon, other young mothers wanted to join. An informal arrangement between two friends soon became the Oholei Yosef Yitzchok (OYY) kindergarten, and then the OYY elementary school, and finally, the OYY school network catering to boys and girls from the ages of two to sixteen.

Gigi Weiss became the headmistress of the school for a while, but as always, her own growing family came first. She soon swapped the leadership job to a part-time teaching role. To supplement their income, the Weiss family took in lodgers. When I first moved to Manchester, I was one of them.

The Weiss family was not the wealthiest in the neighborhood, but the house was permanently filled with the fun and laughter of happy children. Gigi Weiss never had to raise her voice if any of her children did something wrong. Simply having the mother they adored and loved tell them that they had disappointed her was all that was needed.

The loss of a child to a crib death was hard, but Sholom told me that Gigi bore her pain quietly, encouraged by a letter of *chizuk* and *brachah* from the Lubavitcher Rebbe, and she simply carried on with her very busy schedule.

Another Lubavitch innovation for the Manchester community was the establishment of a school for special-needs children called T'mimei Lev. It was started by a wonderful couple, Mr. and Mrs. Gershon Glickman, and of course, Gigi found herself teaching there, too.

Gigi's last teaching post was at the nearby Langdon College, which catered to special-needs Jewish teenagers. Most of the staff, although excellent, were not Jewish and consequently could not properly serve the Jewish needs of the children. Gigi applied for a job there to teach cooking. This was quite a long way from being the prestigious headmistress of a growing Jewish school. It was, though, the foot in the door that she needed to make some changes. The first was to make the kitchen kosher and then to bring it under the supervision of the Manchester Beis Din to make sure that the children would always receive kosher meals. At the same time, she went to night school to acquire qualifications in teaching special-needs children and soon became the head of Jewish studies. A special teacher was now in charge of teaching special *neshamos*.

If all these activities consumed most of Gigi's days, being a trained doula, providing guidance and support to women about to give birth, as well as being a popular *mikveh* attendant, filled many of her nights.

It requires different skills to be a *mikveh* attendant for chassidic ladies than those needed for being in charge of a *mikveh* where many of the women were new to this special mitzvah. Gigi possessed both sets of skills. She was happy to be the woman who opened the door to *frum* ladies on Friday nights, even walking them home if they were nervous. As for her other ladies, those new to this crucial Torah requirement, she worried that they might slip and forget how important this mitzvah was. To ensure that they were cognizant of their obligations, she was available for them any time, day or night. She sometimes even met women minutes after they arrived at the Manchester airport, and took them straight to the *mikveh*.

But it's the little things that often define a tzaddik or *tzaddekes*, not the big ones. Gigi Weiss had other jobs that no one knew about—or at least that she *meant* no one to know about.

Going to a new mother's home when she heard that the mother wasn't coping with her new baby, and volunteering to look after the new baby while the mother got some sleep, was one of those. When she managed to get the baby to go to sleep, too, Gigi would quietly clean the house, from kitchen to bathrooms, before handing the baby back to the mother and slipping out again.

Whether it was the mitzvah of scrubbing a bath or tidying someone's pantry, it was just as important to her as starting a school.

Sometimes, a young Jewish woman envisages herself married to someone at whose side she will stand while together they do great things for the Jewish people. Some may indeed be given the *zechus* to occupy such a role. Others might even feel their life is unfulfilled if they don't have that *zechus*. As Rav Simcha Zissel Ziv wrote, there is greatness in what appears to be a small and easy mitzvah, or even one that some might consider demeaning, like cleaning someone's floor or bathroom. There is certainly greatness in creating a home that is permanently filled with the laughter and fun of happy children.

The path that Gigi Weiss chose for her *derech Hashem* emphasizes a yearning for the coming of Mashiach. Perhaps it's the many small mitzvos that fill up an "ordinary" life that stand the most chance of hurrying his arrival.

As Gigi Weiss quietly and discreetly added to her total of small mitzvos, she made her life one that was anything but ordinary. And each and every one of those mitzvos would be witnesses to testify in the Heavenly court that Gigi's life was, in fact, a great one.

CHAPTER SEVENTEEN

Miriam: Exemplar of Women's Faith

T HE JEWISH PEOPLE had just witnessed the final chapter of the Exodus from Egypt. Pharaoh's army lay dead and washed up on the shore. They had witnessed the waves opening to welcome the Jewish people fleeing them, and the sea offered safe passage to the Jews, allowing them to reach the other side. Instead of coming to the obvious conclusion—that Someone had engineered the miracle (they had, after all, just experienced ten other ones) and guessing what would happen if they pursued their former slaves—they urged their horses on.

The Vilna Gaon says that of all the astonishing miracles that occurred during the Exodus, this one and the madness of the Egyptians' reaction to it was the most miraculous of all.

That message was not lost on Bnei Yisrael as they stood safely on the shore taking in the aftermath of the Egyptians' folly. The Torah tells us, *Then Moshe and Bnei Yisrael sang this song* (*Shemos* 15:1). Prophetic words of praise filled Moshe's mind, the people repeated them, and they sang the most famous Jewish song of all.

The Torah immediately reports that a second song was sung, this one by the women: *Miriam the prophetess, the sister of Aharon, took the musical instrument called a* tof *in her hand. All the Jewish women followed her, carrying* tupim *and* mecholos (*Shemos* 15:20).

Rashi notes an essential difference between the song of the men and that of the women: The women sang accompanied by musical instruments. Rashi asks where they obtained these instruments, and he supplies an amazing answer:

> The saintly women of that generation were so certain that Hakadosh Baruch Hu would save them through miracles that they brought musical instruments out of Egypt.

The men did not bring instruments with them. Clearly, their level of belief and trust in Hashem did not reach the level of that of the women. Regarding this, Rav Chaim Pinchas Scheinberg states, quoting the *Aruch*:

> Why are women on a higher level when it comes to *emunah* than men? *Emunah* itself is a feminine word. It is something innate to women in a way that it is not innate to men.
>
> (*Derech Emunah U'Bitachon*, p. 70)

Miriam was the leader of the women of her generation. They would constantly seek her guidance and direction. The instruction at the beginning of *Avos*—*get yourself a teacher*—is in the masculine. A man has to seek out a *rav*, which in that generation meant Moshe, while a woman should seek out another woman to guide her, and at that time, Moshe's sister filled that role.

Miriam's birth itself pointed to the fact that a unique soul had come into the world. Her mother, Yocheved, was the daughter of Levi. She was born as the Jewish people crossed the border into Egypt at the start of an exile that would last 210 years. She gave birth to her daughter when she was 124 years old—as the Ramban notes, a much greater miracle than Sarah giving birth to Yitzchak at a mere ninety years old. The girl was named Miriam based on the word *mar*, "bitter," to reflect the bitter enslavement that the Jewish people were experiencing.

At the time, there was a "new" king in Egypt (or perhaps an *old* king with a new attitude). The oppression of the people who had done so much to help Egypt and had saved it from perishing during the famine had begun in earnest. The Jewish people's position was intentionally eroded until they became slaves. They were made to perform backbreaking work whose real purpose was to weaken and break them, to set them apart as a nation of slaves.

Within five years, Miriam and her mother would be told to kill all the male babies as they entered the world. The reason for this appalling slaughter was the little girl called Miriam and a prophecy she had made!

As the oppression increased and the strength to resist it waned among the Jewish people, five-year-old Miriam prophesied that her mother would give birth to a boy who would save the Jewish people. Pharaoh's magicians also foresaw Moshe's birth, and they devised a strategy to thwart Hashem's plan.

As the Ohr Hachaim explains, Miriam and her mother were the leading Jewish midwives. A careful reading of the *pesukim* tells of the nature of Pharaoh's plan:

> The king of Egypt spoke to the Hebrew midwives, one who was named Shifrah and the second who was named Puah. And he spoke to them [saying], "When you deliver the Jewish women, you will look on the birthstool. If it is a boy, then you will put him to death, but if it is a girl, she may live."
>
> (*Shemos* 1:15-16)

The Ohr Hachaim explains that in approaching the two leading midwives of the Jewish people, Pharaoh obviously intended that through them, his instructions would pass to all Jewish midwives. He suggested a way that they could tell whether the unborn child was a boy or a girl *before* the child came into the world, and he instructed them to kill the baby boys at that moment, before they were born. This way they could conceal the infanticide as a stillbirth.

But notice that the Torah says Pharaoh "spoke" to them twice, at the beginning of *pasuk* 15 and again at the beginning of *pasuk* 16. The second *pasuk* is explicit regarding what he said to them, which was his command to kill the baby boys while they were still in the womb. What the first thing he spoke to them about is obscure.

Rav Tzvi Hirsch Faber says that the first thing he said to the midwives was that from now on, Yocheved and Miriam would be called Shifrah and Puah! These were Egyptian names and titles bestowed on them by Pharaoh as a reward for what he fully expected would be their loyalty and obedience to the king in carrying out his orders.

The next *pasuk* makes it clear that Yocheved and Miriam could not be "bought" with offers of titles. Their loyalty and obedience were already pledged to another king—the King of kings—and they refused to carry out Pharaoh's orders.

The Ohr Hachaim explains that they justified their failure to do his will by telling Pharaoh that his plan had "leaked," and the Jewish women suspected them. They summoned the midwives only after they had delivered their children, and the baby had been seen to be alive and well. Their only job was to look after both the mother and child after the delivery, so his plan was undone.

The Midrash says that the Egyptian was the prototype of all future exiles (*Vayikra Rabbah* 13:5). There would be a bit of this exile in all of them. Our survival of the Egyptian exile was a promise that we would survive all the others, too. The responses Klal Yisrael used to survive Egypt then would become the blueprints for surviving the exiles to come.

The tactic of trying to recruit the leaders of the Jewish people to betray their own people and cross over to the enemy's side, as Pharaoh did with Yocheved and Miriam, is one that echoes through all four future exiles—Greece, Babylon, Persia, and Rome. One of the most famous examples occurred over 500 years ago in Spain.

King Ferdinand and Queen Isabella's marriage in 1469 united the various countries of the Iberian Peninsula into the country we call Spain. The king and queen offered the great leader of Spanish Jewry, Don Yitzchak Abarbanel, the ability to stay behind and be excluded from the expulsion (he had, after all, done much to make the Spanish royal couple exceedingly rich by managing their finances). He refused and famously led his people into exile rather than become part of the ruling class that expelled them.

The same offer was made to the Abarbanel's colleague and friend, another great rabbi of the time, Rabbi Avraham Seneor. Like the Abarbanel, he had done much to make Spain rich. Both men had raised funds for an army that finally expelled the last Muslim armies from Spain. Both had managed the taxes and wealth of the country, making it rich. As an old man of eighty, Rabbi Seneor chose a different path from that of the Abarbanel and converted to Christianity, taking the name Fernando Perez Coronel Nunez. As a reward, he was given a Spanish noble name and Spanish titles.

The sincerity of the conversion is much debated, but the king and queen's motives in demanding it were obvious. A Jew of such renown who embraced the authority and beliefs of the people who were oppressing the Jewish people would destroy the morale of the Jews trying to resist that oppression.

The Abarbanel chose the other path—the path that Yocheved and Miriam had established in the first exile—and refused to take that role. His reward was that his Torah is still alive and learned by his grateful people to this day. His title is the greatest crown of all. It is the one mentioned in *Avos* (4:13): *the crown of a good name*, which surpasses all other crowns and titles.

Let's return to Miriam's prophecy and its consequences. As the Gemara reports:

> Amram was the *gadol hador*, the leader of the generation. When Pharaoh decreed that all the boys should be thrown into the Nile, he despaired. He divorced his wife, and all the men followed his lead and divorced their wives. His daughter said to him, "Your actions are harsher than Pharaoh's. He only decreed against the boys, but you have decreed against the boys and the girls. Pharaoh has only decreed in this world, but you have decreed both in this world and in the next. Pharaoh is wicked; therefore, his decree may or may not succeed. You are a tzaddik; therefore, your decree will succeed."
>
> (*Sotah* 12a)

Rashi explains that Miriam was telling her father, "You have ensured that no souls will be born and come into the world. If so, they will not be able to earn their share in *Olam Haba*. Pharaoh has only decreed in this world, but you have decreed both in this world and in the next."

Rav Yitzchak Eizik Sher elaborates on this idea:

> It is only when a soul comes to this world and fuses with a physical body that it will be able to enter *Olam Haba*. This applies even if the fusion occurs only within the womb and the child is stillborn. Since there was a merging of a soul with a body, this is enough to allow it to return and stay in Heaven. The critical element is for it to be here on earth, even for the briefest of times.
>
> (*Leket Sichos Mussar*, p. 149)

This was a truth that Miriam, already a prophetess as a young girl of five, understood, and this is what provoked her to reproach her father. It was a message she conveyed to the women of her generation. It was a message that could only be fully received, understood, and acted upon by those on the highest possible levels of *emunah*.

The Yavetz restates that message in his commentary on *Avos* (3:5):

> Someone who makes *Olam Haba* primary and *Olam Hazeh* secondary will not be troubled by the question of *tzaddik v'ra lo*, of why good people suffer in this world.

This is a level of certainty and trust in Hashem that frankly is beyond me. It was not beyond the Jewish women of Egypt, nor their "*rebbi*," Miriam. Their faith bore fruit beyond their imaginings. As the Midrash tells us:

> Rabbi Yehudah asks: "Who was it who praised Hashem [at the splitting of the sea]? The same boys whom Pharaoh wanted to drown in the river. It was they who recognized Hashem!
>
> "When the Jewish people were in Egypt, and a woman knew that her time to give birth had arrived, she would leave her home and go out to the field and deliver her child there. If a boy was born, she would leave him there in the hands of Hakadosh Baruch Hu, saying, 'Ribono Shel Olam, I have

played my part, and now You must play Yours!'"

Rabbi Yochanan says: "Immediately, Hashem would come and clean and feed the child. When these children grew up, they would return to their parents' home. The parents asked them, 'But who looked after you?' Their sons described a 'young man' who appeared and looked after them. When they came to the Red Sea, they saw the vision of Hashem and exclaimed, *Zeh Keli v'anveihu!*—'This is my G-d and I will glorify Him!' The vision had the same appearance as the young man who had cared for them when they were children."

(*Midrash Rabbah, Shemos* 23:9)

Abandoning their sons after birth paralleled Avraham's willingness to sacrifice his son to Hashem at the *Akeidah*. Rav Yitzchak Eizik Sher goes on to elaborate, and I have to admit that whenever I repeat this in a *shiur*, I have to pause, wait for the lump in my throat to subside, and wipe the tears from my cheeks. He says:

Since they did something that Hashem had not commanded them to do, their act even supersedes the *Akeidah*... When ten years or more had passed, the young men, now grown, returned to their homes in groups. It would be hard to imagine the joy their return generated when the sons entered together and said, "Mommy, Mommy, how have you been? Were you worried about us? Where can we find our father?"

Their father would return from the backbreaking work he had been forced to do all day, and his sons would tell him what had happened to them and how they had been looked after and brought up by a "young man." They would recall that when the Egyptians spotted them and ran to kill them, the earth opened and swallowed them, confounding and baffling their pursuers. When the Egyptians gave up the chase, the ground opened up and allowed them to leave now that they were safe.

And their mothers told them that they were not worried about them at all. They explained that they experienced no discomfort from their pregnancies and no pain when they were born. They had total *emunah* and certainty in Hashem.

This is the *emunah* of a woman. This is the legacy of Miriam.

CHAPTER EIGHTEEN

Mrs. Eva "Bubby" Neumann

WHEN I ARRIVED in Gateshead Yeshivah in 1976, an older *bachur* decided to take me under his wing. The yeshivah was learning *Yevamos*, and Sammy Neumann helped me review and understand difficult bits of the Gemara. I noticed that the name inside his Gemara was not his but that of his older brother, Josh. He had learned the same *sugya* a few years earlier when he was in yeshivah, and the slightly battered volume had been passed on to his younger brother.

It's a funny thing how firm friendships develop through a *chavrusa*. Almost all the discussion and exchange of views is focused on complex Talmudic ideas and very little about general or personal subjects. Still, the friendships one makes over a *blatt Gemara* stand the test of time.

I knew Sammy's family from Manchester. His youngest sister was a classmate and friend of my niece. It was much later, only fourteen years ago, that I got to discover how very special his mother was.

After my late wife passed away and I remarried, my wife left California and came to live in Manchester. My niece's old classmate Leah Bergash (Sammy's sister) and her became fast friends. One Shabbos, we joined Leah and her husband for a meal. As Leah's mother lives with her and her family, we got to enjoy the warm and welcoming personality of Mrs. Eva Neumann.

It was after the meal when we were sitting and schmoozing that Leah mentioned almost casually that her mother had just returned from leading a group of young people to Auschwitz.

Early 1944, at the age of fifteen, was the first time she had entered that place. "Bubby" Neumann's grandson, who worked for Aish HaTorah, had persuaded her to return there. Her task was to tell her story to a group of Jews in imminent danger of severing their attachment to the Jewish people and help prevent them becoming lost.

I asked her recently where she got the courage to walk in that accursed place again. She smiled and told me that when she did so, she almost burst into laughter!

"It was such a joke. They have made it look so beautiful—a tourist attraction, making lots of money for the Polish economy." Then she added, "So much green grass now, but no smoke, flames, or screaming."

A momentary shadow crossed her face before she went on to say, "If it would help stop the young people marrying out, I couldn't refuse. And in any case, I could not refuse my grandson anything!" With the mention of his name, her signature smile returned.

Then, Bubby Neumann told us about something that occurred on that trip that was beyond astonishing. The group, along with Eva, entered a room in the camp museum, where she was scheduled to tell her story.

The room had been altered one week before. A unique set of photographs, which had been taken by an SS murderer, recorded in precise detail the arrival of a transport to the death camp. They now hung on the walls.

Eighty or perhaps a hundred souls crammed into each cattle truck spill onto the ground. Screams, blows, and confusion ensue as *kapos* and SS officers arrange them in the ominous order that will lead some to slavery and others to the crematorium. The photographer shows the Jews being tattooed and having their hair shorn. Eventually, those allowed to live a little longer, now in striped pajamas, are marched to barracks and are then assigned backbreaking and soul-destroying tasks.

Each scene captured by the camera's lens was now blown up into huge pictures and fixed in chronological order. Bubby Neumann entered the room with the group of kids, and the then seventy-eight-year-old survivor looked at the display on the wall. Her fifteen-year-old self looked back.

The SS photographer had captured Eva and her cousin's arrival. She was there, being selected, tattooed, shorn, and marched away. Some went straight to their deaths, and some, like Eva, to slave labor, beatings, and starvation.

Those photos were also published in a book called *The Auschwitz Album: The Story of a Transport.* It lay on a table in front of us, and Leah passed it to me.

When you try to look at some landmark or person far off in the distance, your eyes strain and the details are vague. It was like that as I peered at those black-and-white pictures. Looking up at Bubby Neumann, I realized that not only had I not comprehended or understood the enormity of her story, I never could.

Mrs. Neumann told me about her upbringing in Salava, which sometimes belonged to Hungary and sometimes to Czechoslovakia and then Hungary again. Eva was one of three children, and her family, the Birnbaums, were comfortable and very happy. They owned a small hotel and spa, and the Belzer Rebbe, Reb Ahrele, used to come and spend Shabbos in the Birnbaums' home.

The town was over fifty percent Jewish, and even the non-Jews spoke Yiddish. There was only a non-Jewish school for secular studies, but with so many Jews and a Beis Yaakov for Torah studies after the secular day ended, the *frum* community managed very well.

Eva could recall no anti-Semitism at all growing up—until the Nazis invaded Czechoslovakia, that is. The town and territory taken from Hungary was soon returned to the Nazis' fascist allies. Townspeople who had been the Jews' best friends became their bitter enemies.

The slow erosion of the Jews' security and optimism abruptly ended after the last Seder night in 1944. Black-shirted Hungarian Nazis arrived in Salava, and the Jews were ordered to leave their homes, taking no more than one suitcase each. They traveled to Munkacz and from there to the cattle trucks that would take them to Auschwitz, and all along the way, their journey was faithfully recorded by the meticulous Nazi photographer.

The camera only records glimpses of the events that occurred when Eva and her family arrived in Gehinnom. You can't hear the shouts or shots. You can't see her standing one moment surrounded by her family and the next alone, looking desperately for her parents and brothers. The pictures don't reveal her mother and brothers being taken straight to the gas chambers or, in the confusion, the chance meeting with her father, who was unaware of what had happened. You can't hear him telling his daughter, "Be strong. Be *frum*! You must survive to look after your two brothers."

There is too little room here to record Eva's awful months in the camp, including the moment she found her own mother's possessions as she was sorting the belongings of those who had just been gassed. Nor have I space to tell you what happened when she met her grandmother on her way to being gassed, and her grandmother asked her, "Where is your mother?"

Eva survived the death march, and when her typhus-ridden body slipped off a pile of corpses, a Russian officer noticed she was still alive and carried her to a hospital, where he revealed to her in Yiddish that he was a Jew. He arranged for her to wear an armband that declared in Cyrillic that she had typhus. This protected her from Russian soldiers who targeted women.

She told me, "People ask me all the time, 'Where was God in Auschwitz?' I look at them and I tell them, 'Where was God in Auschwitz? He was with me...He was with me.'"

Her journey from the war led her to Budapest, Vienna, and Geneva. She found her husband there, and eventually, they moved to Manchester, where they raised their family; they had two sons and three daughters.

Eva fulfilled her *tatty's* final words: "Be strong! Be *frum*! You must survive to look after your two brothers." She is stronger than anyone I've ever known. She survived to look after two brothers, her own children, and her many grandchildren.

As for the demand that she remain "*frum*," Bubby Neumann told me she was busy planning, at age eighty-eight, the next visit with young non-religious men and women to stop them from becoming lost to Klal Yisrael.

When we stop to wonder how it is possible that Miriam, even as a child born into a world where the Egyptians killed every second Jewish baby, still reached the highest heights of *emunah* in Hashem, allow me to introduce to you one of her daughters and *talmidos*, Eva Neumann.

CHAPTER NINETEEN

Tzipporah: The Other Half of Moshe's Soul

T HE STORY OF Tzipporah is one steeped in the deepest kabbalistic mysteries, and at the same time, it touches the most down-to-earth aspects of womanhood and marriage.

We first meet her in the Torah when she and her six sisters are facing assault and death by drowning at the hands of the Midianite shepherds. Moshe intervenes and is rewarded by her father, Yisro, with a meal, but upon learning that Moshe is a fugitive from Pharaoh, Yisro immediately has him thrown into jail for ten years. Yisro is quite happy to leave him there to die of starvation. We will see later how Tzipporah visited him secretly while he was in jail and brought him food. Eventually, they marry, and she bears him two sons.

The Midrash says that Tzipporah reached the level of all the *Imahos*. When the *pasuk* refers to her as a Cushite, an African (although she was actually a Midianite), Rashi and countless other commentators say that the description refers to her physical beauty and her internal beauty, too. As Rashi puts it, everyone acknowledged her beauty as everyone acknowledges a Cushite's blackness (*Bamidbar* 12:1).

The Midrash further states that she was called Tzipporah because it was she who removed all *avodah zarah* from her father's house (*Vayikra Rabbah* 29). A *tzippor*, or dove, is brought as a sacrifice to remove *tzara'as* from a person, and as long as he is afflicted with it, he is considered as though he is dead. By removing the *avodah zarah* from her father's home, which is known as "*zivchei meisim*," literally, "offerings to the dead" (*Bartenura, Avos* 3:3), she purged and cured it of the cancerous effect the idols were having, much like the offering brings about the removal of *tzara'as*. This gained her the name Tzipporah.

The shepherds' attack on Tzipporah and her sisters occurred precisely because their father had rejected *avodah zarah*. This occurred before Moshe even appeared on his doorstep. Yisro was not the only one in his household to have rejected idolatry. His daughters, particularly Tzipporah, had rejected it, too. And it was she, not Yisro, who completed the family's transformation. She cleared and severed the last ties to *avodah zarah* from the family home.

One is left wondering where she attained the ability to reach such spiritual heights. The answer is twofold: from her first husband, Moshe…and from her second husband, Moshe!

This leads us to revisit something we learned in our exploration of the other righteous women discussed in the previous chapters.

The *Zohar* tells us that Moshe was a *gilgul* of Hevel. The Shem Mi'Shmuel explains why Kayin was the one to suggest the idea of bringing an offering to Hashem, and Hevel only followed Kayin's lead. Kayin was a doer and a fixer. He liked to innovate and create new things. His very name suggests that nature. It relates to the word *kinyan*, which means "acquisition," where an object, person, or thing changes ownership and status. Kayin wanted to bring change to the brand-new world into which he had been born.

Of course, innovation and change can be a very positive thing. However, there is an innate danger when someone is a fixer. He feels pride in the changes he makes, and as a consequence, his ego expands. We have seen how toxic that process is to the human condition and also how men are far more susceptible to its toxicity than women.

The symptoms of the "condition" appeared immediately. True, Kayin came up with the idea, but he brought an offering that was basic, minimal, and grudging. He wanted to keep the best "stuff" for himself. His attitude was that "I" need it.

Hevel's offering was the opposite, a product of his nature. His character was humility. He did not try to alter things even though the change might be positive. That approach was not in his being, which was innately averse to the danger of expanding his sense of self. He was happy to follow his brother's lead and so offered the very best of his property to Hashem. Hevel's attitude was "Why do 'I' need the best?"

Obviously, both approaches, both attributes, have positive and negative aspects.

Hevel's humility played a part in his tragic demise and in evoking his brother's jealousy. Kayin's ego created that jealousy and led to murder.

The kabbalistic texts explain that Hevel was reincarnated as Moshe, whose defining characteristic was humility. This second time, though, Hevel/Moshe would get the balance of his innate character right.

The Torah tells us, *And the man Moshe was exceedingly humble, more than any man on the face of the earth* (*Bamidbar* 12:3). Yet Moshe did not allow his humility to prevent him from acting and "fixing" things. He fixed the enslavement of his people in Egypt. He fixed their inability to leave. He saw to it that they stood at Mount Sinai and received the Torah, and he repeatedly fixed things when they angered Hashem through the golden calf and the spies and on many other occasions.

Kayin was reincarnated as Yisro. The Midrash points to one of the seven names by which Yisro was known, Keini, indicating that he was a descendant of Kayin (*Shemos Rabbah* 27:8). In fact, he *was* the reincarnated Kayin. Like Moshe, Yisro was brought to the world to repair the mistakes he made in a previous life. He was here to be the fixer who did not become poisoned by ego through the fact that he fixed and innovated something.

This is the key to understanding Yisro and why, despite his greatness, his daughter Tzipporah superseded him.

In *Parshas Yisro*, Rashi explains what finally provoked Yisro to embrace the Torah and join Klal Yisrael. This was something that he had not yet done, though he had Moshe as a son-in-law to teach and influence him. The Torah states, *Yisro, the priest of Midian, the father-in-law of Moshe, heard everything that Hashem had done for Moshe and Yisrael, His people* (*Shemos* 18:1).

Rashi clarifies to what the *pasuk* is referring: *What was it that Yisro heard that caused him to come? He heard about the splitting of the Red Sea and the war with Amalek.*

Rashi's answer presents a puzzle. It's easy to imagine Yisro hearing about the miraculous victory Hashem gave the Jewish people at the Red Sea and, as a result, wanting to join such a people. It's not so easy to see how he would reach the same conclusion after hearing about the war with Amalek.

In that war, Bnei Yisrael only just emerged victorious. Moshe climbed to a high spot overlooking the battle. When he raised his hands, Bnei Yisrael saw it, and this caused the Jewish soldiers to connect to Heaven so that they won. When his hands fell, indicating that they had disconnected from Heaven, they started to experience defeat and had to retreat. Eventually, Moshe could no longer keep his hands aloft, and he had to be helped to do so.

The Jewish people won the narrowest of victories, and yet Rashi insists that both events were needed to make Yisro want to embrace Torah. A cynic might say that after such a victory, Yisro might equally have considered joining Amalek. The Alshich explains that when he heard about what happened in the battle against Amalek, he saw something that was the missing piece of the puzzle he needed to make that monumental step. Bnei Yisrael's success was not only about Moshe! He couldn't even keep his hands aloft to guarantee them victory. It was they themselves who had to do that. Each Jew had a role and part to play. To the Kayin in Yisro, this was precisely the ingredient he needed. His nature made him a doer and an innovator. He saw that Bnei Yisrael needed "fixers." And we see that almost as soon as he arrived, he set about fixing things, telling Moshe that he should introduce an innovation in judging the people by bringing in other judges under him, which would relieve him of the entire burden.

Tzipporah was, as the Shelah puts it, "Moshe's missing rib"—the other half of his soul. She had been the other half of his soul when he was here as Hevel, too. Tzipporah complemented Hevel's mission and purpose perfectly. Like a counterweight, Moshe's humility had to be balanced by a "fixer." She failed to fill that role for him when he was Hevel. She reflected and complemented it perfectly again, when she would marry him again, this time as Moshe.

Both Tzipporah and her father had exposure to Moshe over the forty years he lived with them. She had the added advantage of meeting with him and learning from him every day when she secretly brought him the food that kept him alive in prison. She also had another advantage over her father: She was a woman. She did not have the burning desire to be at the forefront of change and innovation. She was not motivated by her sense of "I" and so was not endangered by it.

Chazal don't record what Moshe and Tzipporah discussed in their countless conversations, but certainly, they were discussions and exchanges of insights at the deepest levels. She was, after all, the other half of his soul, and her role was to bring the essential woman's insights to Moshe's perspective and journey.

Harav Samson Raphael Hirsch explains that the Mishnah's statement, *Do not engage in too much conversation with a woman*, refers to one's own "woman," one's wife (*Avos* 1:5). Harav Hirsch clarifies that the word *sichah*, "conversation," connotes shallow and superficial conversation. The Mishnah is therefore telling us that one's wife is far too valuable a resource to squander the opportunities to discuss deep and important matters with her.

Each half of one soul contributes its way of seeing things and completes the other. Tzipporah was the other half of Moshe. Perhaps the reason why *Chazal* do not relate their conversations together is because they were on such an exalted level that we wouldn't be able to fathom what he told her and what she told him.

In the end, it was she who completed the process of purging her father's house of the last vestiges of *avodah zarah*, something Yisro had not done. He could not totally abandon them until he had found something he could embrace instead. That something would have to present him with the opportunity to make a contribution and innovate. When he found that role with Bnei Yisrael and the Torah, he embraced it at once.

Tzipporah, with her innate femininity, had no need for such a center-stage role. Nor did her husband, who spent a week struggling to persuade Hashem to let his brother, Aharon, play that part instead of him. Yet it was that denial of self, the minimizing of his sense of "I," that would allow him to reach the highest heights of any human being since Adam Harishon. As we mentioned above (in Chapter Two), he is referred to as the "daughter of the King," not the "son of the King." At the highest level, where his sense of "I" was so diminished, Moshe embodied a feminine approach, the one that Tzipporah naturally had.

CHAPTER TWENTY

Tzipporah: Beyond This World but of This World

THERE IS A second and essential aspect to uncover in our understanding of Tzipporah.

I recall the first time I met my *rosh yeshivah*, Rav Leib Gurwicz. I had come to Gateshead for a *bechinah* to see if I could be accepted into the yeshivah. After the *farher*, he turned to me and asked, "Can I make you a cup of tea?" Rav Leib, one of the *gedolei hador*, then left to go into the kitchen, and when he returned, he carried a tray with a teapot, sugar, milk, fruit, and biscuits and one of the warmest and kindest smiles I had ever seen.

I told this story to a friend (who would go on to become my brother-in-law), and he said, "Ah, yes. Reb Leib is great enough to be normal."

In the biography of Rav Nosson Tzvi Finkel, the same observation was made about him. In my many interactions with *chassidishe* rebbes, too, the same fact emerges: Holiness, even at the highest levels, does not preclude normalcy and sensitivity to the realities of human behavior.

At the end of *Parshas Beha'aloscha*, the Torah recalls an upsetting incident regarding Tzipporah:

> Miriam and Aharon spoke regarding the Cushite woman
> that Moshe had married because he had married a Cushite
> woman.
>
> (*Bamidbar* 12:1)

Rashi questions why the Torah says Tzipporah was a Cushite woman when she wasn't, and more, why it uses the term twice in the same *pasuk*. Rashi goes on to explain:

> Everyone acknowledged that her beauty was as indisputable as the fact that an African's skin is black. The numerical value of the word "Kushis" is the same as that of *yefas mareh*, "beautiful appearance"... [The reason it repeats the term "Kushis" twice is that] you might find a woman whose appearance is beautiful, but her behavior is unpleasant, and others whose behavior is beautiful, but whose appearance is plain. Tzipporah was beautiful in every respect.

The theme of feminine beauty is expounded in the *Sifri's* answer to the question of what caused Miriam and Aharon to be discussing Tzipporah and, as we learn from Rashi, the fact that Moshe separated from his wife:

> How did they know that he had separated from normal married life? Miriam noticed at that time that Tzipporah no longer wore the jewelry that married women wear. She asked her sister-in-law, "Why do you no longer wear jewelry like other married women?" She replied, "Your brother is no longer particular about my need to wear it." From that comment, Miriam understood that Moshe had abandoned normal married life.

The Gemara says that Moshe had concluded that he needed to separate himself from his wife from a *kal vachomer* (*Shabbos* 87a). He calculated, "If the Jewish people who stood at Mount Sinai to come face-to-face with Hashem had to separate from their wives three days beforehand, then how much more so must I, who can be called to appear before Hashem at any time without warning, separate from my wife."

We can infer, then, that before that time and necessity, Moshe *was* particular that his wife should wear jewelry and appear beautiful.

The Gemara tells a story about one of the most remarkable Sages of the Gemara (*Ta'anis* 23b). His name was Abba Chilkiyah. He was the grandson of Choni Hame'agal, and like his grandfather, this holy man had the ability to change the decree of Heaven whenever it was harsh, as in times of drought. On one occasion, two Sages were dispatched by the Sanhedrin to ask Abba Chilkiyah to pray for rain. They accompanied him as he returned home and noticed that his wife came out to meet him wearing jewelry. When he entered his house, he let his wife enter first while they entered last. Later, the Sages asked him to explain the reason for these and other perplexing behaviors they had observed.

"When the Rav reached the town," they asked, "why did his wife come out to greet him wearing jewelry?"

He answered frankly. "She did so in order that my eyes should not stray and look at any other woman."

"Why did you allow your wife to enter first and you followed her?" they asked.

He replied, "Because I do not know you well!"

Rashi explains that because he didn't know their character, he didn't want his wife to be alone with them in the street even for a few seconds.

Both Abba Chilkiyah and his wife prayed for rain, and their prayers were answered. Interestingly, her prayers were answered before his. Both were possibly the holiest people of their entire generation and the only ones who could change Heaven's decree, and yet both were aware of their duty as a spouse to protect each other. Abba Chilkiyah was on his guard against any man who might behave inappropriately toward his wife. She was on her guard to make sure that she made herself the focus of his interest and took care to enhance her beauty and appearance.

Even at the highest levels, tzaddikim, male and female, are not unaware of the requirements of a husband and a wife toward one another. Holiness does not preclude sensitivity to the realities of human behavior. Before Moshe found himself in his unique situation, he expected his wife to enhance her beauty as any wife should. She was happy to do so and understood that it was part of her role to fulfill that expectation.

One of my greatest teachers was Rav Alter Halpern, the *rosh yeshivah* of Toras Emes in London. He once offered me a definition of *tznius* as it applies to girls:

A girl has to broadcast in the way that she dresses and the way that she acts that she is attractive and available—but only to the right man in the right circumstances. That is to say, not to the right man under the wrong *circumstances and not to the wrong man under any circumstances.*

There is another aspect of the well-known story of Miriam talking to Aharon about Moshe separating from his wife. The consequence of the story was, of course, that Miriam was afflicted with *tzara'as* for speaking *lashon hara*. This led me to wonder why, in repeating the words of Tzipporah that revealed her separation from Moshe, Miriam suffered *tzara'as* but Tzipporah didn't.

Of course, you could say that Miriam had to deduce from Tzipporah's words what her situation was. She did not actually say it explicitly. But there are *midrashim* that describe other events that led to the secret being revealed.

After the rebellion with regard to the manna, when the people complained about their lack of meat, Hashem told Moshe to select seventy elders who could share the burden of leadership with him:

> Hashem said to Moshe, "Gather for Me seventy men among the wise men of Israel whom you know to be the wise ones of the people and their officers and take them to the Mishkan, and they will stand there with you. I will come down and speak with you there, and I will increase the spirit that is on you and bestow it on them."
>
> (*Bamidbar* 11:16-17)

The *Yalkut Shimoni* comments:

> When the elders were appointed, the entire Jewish nation lit lights and celebrated with them. Miriam saw the lights and said to Tzipporah, "Why are those lights lit?" Tzipporah explained the reason.

Miriam exclaimed, "Happy are the wives of these seventy men that they have seen how their husbands have been promoted to such positions of authority!"

Tzipporah said, "Woe to these women! From now on, their husbands will have no physical contact with them, and they will be childless from this point onward."

Miriam asked, "How can you be sure?"

Tzipporah replied, "From your brother. From the moment that he was aware that Hashem could speak to him at any time, he has not entered my room."

Hearing that, Miriam hurried to Aharon to tell him what she had heard.

In this version of events, Tzipporah actively revealed what Moshe had done. And so, we return to our question: If Miriam was punished for uttering these words, why wasn't Tzipporah punished?

One answer can be found in *sefer Chafetz Chaim* (*Lashon Hara* 10). There, the Chafetz Chaim discusses circumstances in which it may be possible to speak *lashon hara*—for example, if you are doing so to warn someone about a person with whom they are thinking of going into business because you know that the person is dishonest. The Chafetz Chaim takes great pains to stress the rigorous rules that apply in such a case in order to guarantee that the permission to speak is not abused nor becomes corrupted into becoming an excuse to speak forbidden *lashon hara*.

He goes on to state:

> In employing this *heter*, you must be completely sure that you are motivated solely to produce a positive outcome [and not to harm the person you are speaking about]. This is the foundation upon which this exception to the prohibition of speaking negatively about another Jew is built.
>
> (*Chafetz Chaim, Lashon Hara* 14)

In an addendum on the same page, the Chafetz Chaim adds:

> It is possible that it is also permitted if you are saying the *lashon hara* to lessen the real pain the incident you are

reporting is causing you. That is what *Chazal* (*Yoma* 75a) mean when they interpret the *pasuk*, *If there is pain in a person's heart, let him tell it to others* (*Mishlei* 12:25). However, in doing so, one must be rigorous not to contravene any of the conditions outlined above.

In the Dirshu edition of the *sefer Chafetz Chaim*, many opinions of the *poskim* are cited in discussing this *heter*. Here is what Rav Yitzchak Hutner and Rav Shlomo Zalman Auerbach have to say about a woman who is very upset about something that has happened and comes to report it to her husband:

> It is a husband's duty to listen when his wife is upset and to calm her from her distress or things that have caused her anxiety. It is therefore obvious that it is not forbidden for her to bring her pain and story to her husband.

Along the same lines, *Sefer Chassidim* states the following regarding someone who comes to you in distress to tell you of his pain:

> When they come seeking relief from their pain, it is a mitzvah to listen to them. If possible, you should then seek to remedy the problem and bring about a reconciliation between the person who is speaking to you and the one he is speaking about. However, if the person reporting his situation to you is also repeating the same story to others, then they are not motivated by seeking "therapy" for their anguish but by *motzi shem ra*, the wish to spread unfounded gossip. Upon discovering that this is their real agenda, you should make your anger at this clear. To calm your distress and find healing, almost always, one person is sufficient.
>
> (*Sefer Chassidim*, ch. 64)

From the account of the *Yalkut Shimoni*, we can see that Tzipporah was in real pain on behalf of the seventy women who were about to share her painful experience. She said, *Woe to these women! From now on, their husbands will have no physical contact with them, and they will be childless from this day forward!*

She was clearly still in pain, too. As we said before, the greatest and holiest man or woman nevertheless remains a man or woman. They are still human.

As mentioned above, Rav Dessler points out that when the great Nachum Ish Gamzu always reacted to bad news with his iconic expression *gam zu l'tovah*—"This, too, is for good," he was expressing how he saw catastrophe and suffering in his mind. In his heart, though, he still felt the pain and was in no way excluded from the obligation to utter the words everyone does upon hearing bad news: "*Baruch Dayan Ha'emes.*"

In confiding her pain to Miriam, Tzipporah was bearing her pain to the person who occupied the leadership role among the women of Klal Yisrael that Moshe did among the men, and she fulfilled all the conditions that the Chafetz Chaim stipulated, sharing it with no one but Miriam. She was also telling someone who was in a position to act and perhaps do something to ease her pain.

The mistake Miriam made was in not going to the person about whom she had just been told information. Instead, she went to his brother, Aharon. The Torah and *Chazal* offer many insights into what happened next. Tzipporah, though, suffered no criticism for sharing her pain with the one person who could help.

CHAPTER TWENTY-ONE

Rebbetzin Liba Gottlieb

BEFORE THE SECOND World War, America was a seductive and confusing place for the Jews who had left "*Der Heim*" behind and arrived to make the United States their new home. I once heard the Novominsker Rebbe say in a *shiur* that if they ever dredge the Hudson River, they will find thousands of pairs of *tefillin* lying at the bottom.

When Jews stood at the bow of the ships that brought them to the end of their transatlantic sea voyage, they gazed up at the famous giant green statue, which was both a symbol and a promise that had drawn them to these shores. They had to bend their necks back even further to take in the even more gigantic buildings that lived up to the name skyscraper and truly towered to the sky.

This was clearly a new world, very different from the one they left behind. What place did the ancient customs and practices of the Old World have in this new one? Thousands who fell for the lie that the "sidewalks were paved with gold" fell for the other lie that they didn't have to hold on to the Torah and "arcane" items like *tefillin*. For many, if not most, both were soon discarded and thrown away.

Rebbetzin Liba Gottlieb's father arrived in America in a more unconventional way. He left Poland and initially landed in Canada. From there, Nechemia Millar eventually crossed over the border to pursue the American dream in the "*goldene medinah.*"

Perhaps there was a hint in his unusual route to an American Jewish life that would itself be unusual. But that would reveal itself many years later, when he had established himself in Boston as the manager of a shoe factory and started to build his family.

His wife's family had arrived from the old country amid an earlier wave of immigrants, and Chana Leah was born in the U.S. Together, they had two daughters. If others had thrown their Jewish identity away, Liba Gottlieb's father and mother had not. The family were traditional Jews. If precise observance of the halachah did not govern their lives, the values they represented did.

Liba's father sent his two girls to Boston's Maimonides School, which was founded in 1937 by Rav Yosef Ber Soloveitchik. To seek a Torah education for your daughters in those days was almost unheard of, but then again, we already established that Rebbetzin Gottlieb's father was a rather unusual Jew.

Perhaps he was encouraged in his decision when his daughter Liba seemed to want to extend the family's traditional Jewish lifestyle to one that adhered to halachah completely. Even as a young girl of six or seven, her family's nickname for her was "The Rebbetzin." Interesting, too, was the fact that her father did not object to her efforts and actually encouraged her journey toward *shemiras hamitzvos.* He once told her, "Pursue your religious goals, but make sure you do it properly—without compromises or half measures!"

If his heart had a flaw, it was in the physical sphere as opposed to the spiritual one. He was advised by his cardiologist to move to Florida, where the warm weather would help his heart condition. Liba's father, along with his wife and girls, packed and shipped their possessions south to the Sunshine State. The four Millars followed by train. During that journey, tragedy struck. Nechemia Millar's heart stopped beating for good. Chana Leah Millar and her two daughters arrived in Florida to start their new life and immediately had to arrange a funeral.

From then on, Liba had to attend a very different kind of school from the one she had attended in Boston. Her new school was an

American public school. It provided a perfect education for Jews who believed that the Torah was "irrelevant and arcane." It was anathema to a girl whose nickname was "The Rebbetzin." And yet, somehow, after her years attending public school, Liba emerged much stronger in her beliefs and convictions than before.

After high school, Liba Millar moved back to the Boston area to attend Brandeis University and work toward earning a degree in sociology. It was there that she met a brilliant young man who was studying philosophy. They discovered that they had an uncanny amount in common. Both had one sibling—she had a sister, he had a brother. Both were born ten years apart from that sibling. There was ten years' difference in their parents' ages, and both were the eldest in their families. They were also both nurturing their commitment and growth in Torah.

The match was obvious to both of them, but there was one significant obstacle in the way. Liba was passionate about settling in Eretz Yisrael, and she shared with her would-be *chassan* this pivotal factor upon the proposed engagement.

Anyone who has heard a *shiur* from Rabbi Gottlieb will know that logic is fundamental to the way his mind works and the conclusions at which he arrives. He told his would-be *kallah* that he would honestly find it difficult to agree to such an undertaking since he had never actually been to the Holy Land. The logical thing to do, of course, was to go there and see if he could share her passion and remove the obstacle.

Dovid Gottlieb set off to learn in Yeshivas Merkaz HaRav in Yerushalayim, where all the *shiurim* were in Hebrew. Rabbi Gottlieb claims that languages are a weakness of his (having known him as a close friend, alongside whom I have taught many times for some thirty-five years, I must admit to some skepticism on that point). Within a few months of hearing *shiurim* exclusively in Hebrew, he attained fluency in the language and fell deeply in love with Eretz Yisrael.

He dispatched a note to his Liba to tell her, "You can consider yourself formally engaged!" He had a *l'chaim* and small celebration with his friends and *chavrusos* in Yerushalayim, and Liba had a parallel celebration with her girlfriends in Boston.

Marriage soon followed, along with the arrival of three children, but their dream of moving to Eretz Yisrael would have to wait while Dovid Gottlieb achieved his PhD at Brandeis. During that period, Liba balanced motherhood with teaching in her old school, Maimonides.

There were many things they would share and give to each other. Rabbi Gottlieb is renowned for his remarkable intellect. He considered his wife to be similarly bright. "She had a broad perspective on things and saw the big picture," he told me. "My mind is more narrowly focused, zooming in to analyze and dissect a problem."

He offered me an intriguing example of how his late wife's mind worked. Rebbetzin Gottlieb once pointed out that Klal Yisrael's greatness and uniqueness was demonstrated when they stood at Mount Sinai and declared, *Na'aseh v'nishma*—"We undertake to practice the Torah and afterward we will hear how we must practice it." It was an unquestioning acceptance of Hashem's will. She then posed a question to her husband: "Where do we find an example of Moshe himself expressing an unquestioning acceptance of Hashem's will in the same way?"

In fact, she continued, the Torah records countless times when Moshe asked Hashem for an explanation, such as when he said, *Why have You done bad to this people?* (*Shemos* 5:22). He struggled with Hashem when He announced He was going to eradicate Bnei Yisrael after the sin with the golden calf (*Shabbos* 32a) and again after the spies brought back their report.

It seems that struggling against Heaven's decree was the theme of Moshe's life.

It was a question Rabbi Gottlieb could not answer and one that also excited him. He took it to several *gedolei Torah*, who similarly could not offer a solution to his wife's question.

On another occasion, she once asked her husband how long it took him to walk from college to his car. He replied that it was a walk of around twenty minutes. She asked him what he saw during those walks and to describe it to her.

Her new husband was baffled. He didn't recall *anything* from his walks, though he took the same walk every single day.

She suggested that he consider looking at the grass, flowers, and trees. She told him to look at the birds and listen to their songs. Perhaps he might notice the architecture of the buildings he passed by and question whether or not they were well designed. In his turn, as an accomplished flautist, he introduced his wife to the world of music and other disciplines like science to which *his* mind was attuned.

More crucial in building their marriage was how they complemented each other in Torah, sharing questions like the one above and exchanging insights and discoveries regarding a *pasuk* or statement of *Chazal*.

Still, the move to Eretz Yisrael had to wait when Rabbi Gottlieb became a professor of philosophy at Johns Hopkins University and the couple moved to Baltimore. There, Rebbetzin Gottlieb worked for various organizations, putting her social work degree to good use in the field of *chessed*. She counseled those who were unemployed in how to present and express themselves when applying for a job. She worked with the institute for the blind and shared her insights and wisdom in other areas with those who needed it most.

When my late wife was first diagnosed with the illness that she fought for five years, I received a phone call from Rebbetzin Gottlieb. She offered me a piece of advice that was a lifesaver at the time. I subsequently shared it with others, and it produced the same therapeutic effect.

She began with a preamble: "Some really nice and good people are going to say lots of really stupid things to you now." She let that thought sink in and then continued, "Instead of getting upset, when someone says something tactless, insensitive, or hurtful—keep an idiot book!"

She told me to make a note (at least mentally) of all the inappropriate things people told me, and instead of them making me upset, they would generate a tiny smile, knowing that they were about to be added to the book.

Eventually, after a fifteen-year detour in Baltimore, the Gottliebs moved to Eretz Yisrael, the place that Rebbetzin Gottlieb had always been passionate about and that Rabbi Gottlieb set out to discover and fell in love with. Rabbi Gottlieb started giving *shiurim* at Yeshivas Ohr Somayach, where he teaches to this day, while his *rebbetzin* worked for several organizations that were desperate for her skills and wisdom.

One of those was Sulam, an organization that provided educational services and therapy for *chareidi* families with children born with Down syndrome and other similar conditions. She even fundraised for the organization in America and England. More than this, she played an important role in campaigning to remove the stigma and embarrassment that some parents felt at having a child with these special needs.

After her passing, her husband suddenly found himself immersed in a rising tide of letters and emails from people who wanted to tell him of acts of remarkable *chessed* they had received at the hands of his wife. In some cases, their situation had been desperate before her intervention. In most cases, he knew absolutely nothing about the stories he read. Liba simply hadn't shared them with him.

"Imagine," he said, "you're walking down a street, and as you pass an old person or a child, they start to fall. What would you do? Obviously and naturally, you would grab hold of them if you can stop them falling. It is a reaction so natural that you wouldn't see anything out of the ordinary in your reaction or the help you gave. That is how my late wife looked at all the people she helped. They were falling. She simply reached out to stop it happening. There was nothing exceptional in that as far as she was concerned and nothing to report."

There is, though, much to report and learn from the life of someone who enjoyed the affectionate nickname of "The Rebbetzin" by her family as a very little girl. She overcame a devastating tragedy and proved impervious to a negative environment, going on to earn her nickname in actuality.

There is also much to learn from a woman who shared her perspectives, wisdom, and understanding with her husband and helped him grow while learning from his wisdom and growing from it, too.

CHAPTER TWENTY-TWO

Rachav: Listening and Believing

THE CANAANITE GIRL was ten years old when something happened that reverberated around the world. Everyone knew about the event, and everyone was terrified by what it meant. It was clear that nothing would ever be the same again, but then, as time passed, people put it out of their minds and forgot all about it and its message.

There were two individuals, though, who didn't forget. One was Yisro—and the other was that little girl.

The event was Bnei Yisrael's Exodus from Egypt. As the Midrash informs us:

> Rachav was only ten years old when Bnei Yisrael left Egypt. For the entire forty years that the Jewish people traveled in the desert, she lived an immoral life. At the end of her fiftieth year, she converted and became a Jew. She said, "Ribono Shel Olam, in three areas, I have sinned: *niddah*, challah, and candle lighting. Because of three things, please forgive me those sins: through the rope, the window, and the wall."
>
> (*Mechilta, Yisro* 1)

"The rope, the window, and the wall" refer to the items that she employed to hide and protect Yehoshua's spies when they entered Eretz Yisrael to scout the region of Yericho.

This midrash is profoundly puzzling. How could she have sinned in those three areas when none of them applied to her? She was not a Jew and therefore had no obligation to keep the laws of *niddah*, challah, or Shabbos candle lighting.

In Chapter Five above, where we explored the life of Rivkah, we saw the Alshich's explanation of these three uniquely female experiences. The role of a woman, any woman, is in how much she has contributed to undoing the damage caused through the part Chavah played in the eating of the *eitz hada'as*. On a mystical level, these three mitzvos repair the damage of that first sin.

That is what Rachav was referring to here, too. She had not fulfilled her role as a woman and a daughter of Chavah to repair that damage until now. But through the three items she used to save Yehoshua's spies, she saved two Jewish lives and asked that this should be her contribution.

In truth, as we shall see, she was saving *much* more. But first we need to ask: How did she achieve this insight and understanding?

To answer this question, we have to return to the life of Yisro. The Torah tells us that after the giving of the Torah, *Yisro, the priest of Midian, the father-in-law of Moshe, heard all that Hashem had done for Moshe and Yisrael, His people* (*Shemos* 18:1).

The Alshich asks why the Torah has to tell us in such detail who Yisro was when the Torah has already told us Yisro's identity when it relates the story of Moshe saving his daughters from the shepherds' attack. We also already know his relationship to Moshe.

The Alshich also points to the inaccuracy of the chronology in the *pasuk*. Yisro received this name after he became a Jew, and he was therefore no longer the idolatrous priest of Midian. If he was "the priest of Midian," he was not Yisro.

The Alshich goes on to answer that the Torah is not dealing with Yisro's chronology; rather, it is considering his methodology. Though he had been an idolatrous priest, he could still become a "Yisro" for the simple reason contained in the first word of his *parshah*: *vayishma*. He listened! The entire world *heard* what Hashem had done for the Jews at the Exodus, but only two people actually *listened*.

Imagine one night you hear a noise from downstairs after the house has been locked for the night. The next thing you do after you hear the noise is to listen for it. One denotes casual hearing and the other concentrating and assessing.

There was an additional factor that aided Yisro's transformation, which is why the Torah emphasizes that he was the father-in-law of Moshe. Yisro was connected to a tzaddik. He had a *rebbi*.

There was one other person who was listening, a woman called Rachav. She, though, did not have a *rebbi*.

How did she achieve what she did? How did she attain greatness? The answer can be found in the words of Rav Chaim Friedlander:

> If a person does not resolve to change himself, how will words of wisdom and insight help? A person can hear the most inspiring and beautiful words and ideas, and they may even enter his or her heart. Unless they act on those words and immediately effect real change within themselves, those words and their message will soon be forgotten. It requires a process where the words are considered and contemplated. They have to be thought about over and over, while delving into every aspect and implication they contain.
>
> (*Sifsei Chaim, Mo'adim*, vol. 1, p. 9)

Rav Yerucham Levovitz says that the reason Rachav's story is read as the *haftorah* for *Parshas Shelach*, the *parshah* of the spies, is not to compare Moshe's spies to Yehoshua's, as you might think—it is to compare them to Rachav (*Da'as Chachmah U'mussar*, vol. 1, p. 9)!

The spies who brought back the negative report about Eretz Yisrael did not merely hear about the splitting of the Red Sea. They witnessed and experienced it. They were also the greatest and best emissaries the Jewish people could send. Yet their mission was disastrous and brought calamity upon Bnei Yisrael.

Compared to these spiritual giants, Rachav's spiritual level was minuscule. But she had taken what she heard about the splitting of the sea and made it part of her very being, thinking about it and adding to it every day. Rachav may have been insignificant compared to the spies, but she was on the way up. They had let the inspiration of the Exodus slip away. These great men had stopped thinking about it and adding to the inspiration they had experienced. They had stopped growing and stood still—and then, they started to fall. Rachav soon caught up with them and then surpassed them:

> When Rachav took the two spies into her house and saved them, Hashem considered it as though she saved Him and consequently rewarded her. This is why the *pasuk* says, *The woman took the two men and hid him (Yehoshua 2:4).*
>
> (*Bamidbar Rabbah* 2:3)

If that was how Hashem viewed what she had done, it should hardly come as a surprise that her reward was immeasurable. The *Sifri* tells us just how vast that reward was:

> Eight *kohanim* and eight prophets descended from Rachav. They were Yirmiyahu, Chilkiyahu, Sariyah, Machsayah, Baruch, Nerya, Chanma'el, and Shalom. Rabbi Yehudah adds that Chuldah the prophetess was also a direct descendant of Rachav.
>
> (*Sifri, Beha'aloscha* 78)

Elsewhere, it is written that she was also the mother of seven Jewish kings (*Tanna D'vei Eliyahu Zuta* 22:3).

Rav Yerucham Levovitz goes on to say:

> In protecting the messengers of the Jewish people, it was as though Rachav had protected the entire Jewish people. Since Hashem always rewards measure for measure, it would not be a surprise that she would be given the merit of having children and descendants who would carry on doing the same thing.
>
> (*Da'as Chachmah U'mussar*, vol. 1)

In a letter to his son, Rav Simcha Zissel Ziv of Kelm expresses his anguish and pain when he had read his son's letter telling him of how much he had suffered during a recent illness. He then goes on to thank Hashem for sending his son a *refuah sheleimah—in order that you will be able to do kindness with the* rov, *the "many," among Klal Yisrael, as you desire.*

He goes on to say:

> What does it mean to benefit the "many"? Rachav did an act of kindness for two people who were acting on behalf of all the Jewish people. She was consequently seen as having helped the entire Jewish people. Otherwise, how could they promise her that no Jew would harm any of her family? This gives us an insight into the enormity of the reward of helping the *klal.*
>
> It also points to the incalculable repercussions of having a clear perspective. The entire world, including the king of Yericho, heard what Hashem had done for Bnei Yisrael from the splitting of the Red Sea until now, but Rachav saw the events with clarity. Let's see what came of seeing the world "clearly."
>
> Rachav had lived a life of immorality for forty years. Yet her clarity elevated her from that life to embrace Torah and to become the wife of a Jew who was the closest in spiritual level to Moshe Rabbeinu—his successor, Yehoshua. And that was still not enough. She also became the mother of *kohanim* and prophets, including Chuldah.
>
> It is astonishing to think how a moment's epiphany that is immediately acted upon can utterly transform a human being. It caused Rachav to do *chessed* with two ambassadors of the Jewish people and subsequently become the wife of the leader of that people. In one moment, she discovered and recognized the *emunah* in Hashem that lay in her heart and knew with total conviction that, *Hashem, your God, He is God in the heavens and on the earth below* (*Yehoshua* 2:11).
>
> She knew her rebellion against the king of Yericho [harboring the two spies and not handing them over] placed her life in immediate danger. But that didn't matter to her if she was saving the ambassadors of Hashem's people.

Now we can see the reward of those who worry on behalf of Klal Yisrael, experiencing their pain as though it is their own, because indeed it is, and they rejoice in the celebrations of others, because these celebrations are their celebrations, too.

Hashem is, of course, limitless. So is every element of Him, including His rewards. And who deserved such rewards more than a woman whose forty years of immorality and turpitude were transformed into merits? As the Gemara says, *In the place that* ba'alei teshuvah *stand, complete tzaddikim are not able to stand* (*Brachos* 34b).

That is the point of the story of Rachav, according to *Chazal*, who echo the words of the *Sifri*: Someone—Rachav—came from a people whom Klal Yisrael were told were so beyond redemption that they had to be completely eradicated. Yet she became close to Hashem. He reciprocated and became close to her. How much more so in the case of Jews who carry out the instructions of the Torah—they, too, come close to Hashem.

If the reward seems remarkably generous, it was given to a woman who was one in a million, or indeed many millions. She was the only woman in the non-Jewish world who paid attention and took her belief and love of Hashem into her heart. She kept it there, and even without a *rebbi* to guide her, pondered it and examined all its facets, adding them to her growing *emunah*. Of course, Hashem's reward reflected her uniqueness: it, too, was unique.

Rose

THE DRAMATIC AND enormous miracles that occurred in Egypt lead us to recognize the little hidden miracles that are the foundation of the entire Torah (since we come to realize that everything, even that which seems natural, comes from Hashem). So writes the Ramban at the end of *Parshas Bo*. And those little hidden miracles, as we say three times daily in *Modim* of the *Shemoneh Esrei*, are "with us *every* day."

Not too long ago, I received a phone call from a *rav* who is involved in the truly remarkable rebirth of Torah and *shemiras hamitzvos* among New York's Bukharan community. He wanted me to come and speak to eighty or so young Jews who had just kept their first Shabbos. That's when I heard about one of those small miracles that remind us that Hashem constantly supervises and controls our world.

Before I spoke, a young lady from Long Island called Rose told her story. She began by explaining that the last Shabbos had been the tenth in a row that she had kept properly. This produced applause from all her listeners.

At first, she explained, she found keeping Shabbos *very* hard. Rose lives at home with her family. She sat through the long Shabbos afternoons surrounded by parents and siblings watching TV or calling and texting on their phones. All this made keeping Shabbos more than tough. After her second Shabbos, Rose announced to her family that she could not continue on in this way. They would have to help her keep Shabbos! She demanded that they play board games with her for one hour after her Shabbos meal.

I have not met any of Rose's family members, but it's clear that they are very special people. They all undertook to help, and the one hour for which they switched off their phones and played card games with her extended to two.

Rose's closeness to her family was tested soon afterward. She had always hoped to get into dental school and had enrolled at St. John's University in Queens to take its pre-dental program. Then came the next big step: applying to the best dental school in New York—Columbia. There are only a few spots available each year, and even getting an interview is a big deal. When Rose received a letter telling her that she had an interview, her family's excitement, especially her father's, was palpable. His daughter securing a career in dentistry, which would set her up for life, would be a dream come true.

The interview went particularly well, and the interviewer, one of the school's senior lecturers, complimented her on her test scores and enthusiasm.

"I am giving a lecture here tomorrow morning at ten," he explained. "I can't exactly promise, but I think I can say with confidence that if I see you at that lecture, you can assume that you will have a place in the school."

Rose's eyes widened, as did her smile, but then the smile faltered. She had just recalled that tomorrow was Shabbos.

Nervously, Rose explained that she observed the Jewish Sabbath and would not be able to attend the lecture. The interviewer simply repeated what he had just said while putting special emphasis on the words, "If you come to the lecture, you can safely assume you will have a place."

Rose returned home and told her parents what had happened. Her father didn't notice the look of sadness in his daughter's eyes. He was too ecstatic about the news that she was only one "ten o'clock lecture" away from her dream career.

"I can't go, Dad," Rose said in a quiet voice. "It's Shabbos."

Her father looked at her in bewilderment. "But, honey, it's your entire career! Surely God won't mind if you break the Sabbath just once in *your entire career.*" Rose answered that she rather thought Hashem probably *would* mind.

As she relayed this story to the eighty Bukharans listening, she admitted that the *yetzer hara* was busy adding its voice to her father's question: *Maybe Hashem wouldn't mind, after all?*

Then her father tried a new tack: "We've put aside some money for you—$3,500. We'll give you that, and you can give it to whichever Jewish charity you like. Now will you go to the lecture?"

The *yetzer hara* was working overtime on the young Jewish woman who had kept only a handful of Shabbosos. The questions multiplied:

Of course, now Hashem won't mind! What if you take an Uber? Surely that's not such a problem according to the halachah?

This is your career we're talking about here! Did you hear your father? $3,500 dollars for tzedakah! *Surely Hashem will be okay with that!*

But deep down, Rose knew the right answer to all her questions. She turned sad eyes to her father and slowly shook her head. "I'm sorry, Dad. I don't think I can go."

Rose and her father are particularly close. She loves him very much, and he knew it. And so he played his trump card: "If you won't do this for yourself—will you do it for *me*?"

Rose didn't go to the lecture and kept Shabbos instead. But by Sunday, she was racked with remorse and doubt. Those questions were back. Perhaps her father was right, after all? Perhaps she'd thrown away her life's ambition for nothing? Maybe Hashem wouldn't have minded if she had gone just that once...

Rose called her new *rebbetzin* and, while crying her eyes out, told her what had happened. The *rebbetzin* listened carefully and with great sensitivity. Then, she reminded the young woman that this was something they had already learned about together. "Sometimes in life," said the *rebbetzin*, "Hashem sends you a test."

The *rebbetzin* conceded that this was a big test and not an easy one to pass, but she *had* passed it.

Rose listened intently through sobs as her *rebbetzin* encouraged her not to regret her choice. Throughout the conversation, Rose was distracted by someone phoning over and over and leaving voicemail messages. Eventually, she couldn't bear the interruptions any longer and explained to her *rebbetzin* that she had to see who was calling and what they wanted that was so important that they kept calling. She disconnected her call with the *rebbetzin* and listened to the voicemail the person had left.

At this point in the presentation to her Bukharan audience, she paused and played them the voicemail that she heard:

"Here is your message. Test, test, test. This is a test. St. John's University public safety. This is only a test."

The message repeated itself over and over until Rose hung up. It was an automated, routine security message to the university's students, the kind they would send if there was a real emergency on campus.

But that message was anything but routine.

In the middle of a conversation where Rose's *rebbetzin* was telling her that Hashem had simply been sending her a test, a small miracle occurred.

This morning, days after hearing this story from Rose, I called her to ask how she was doing and whether she got into dental school. She hadn't heard either way yet, but frankly, she doesn't have to. This remarkable young woman understands the test she was given and the reason for it.

Rose knows it's one of those little miracles that happen *every day* and remind us that Hashem constantly supervises and controls our world.

CHAPTER TWENTY-FOUR

Rus: The Necessity of Having a Rebbetzin

MY GOOD FRIEND Rabbi Moshe Kupetz of Manchester once asked me a question, with a smile playing on his lips: "How rich would a Jew have to be to marry into the British Royal family?"

The question was clearly rhetorical. The answer was, of course, "Fabulously rich!"

This led him to ask a second question every bit as rhetorical as the first: "How rich did Elimelech have to be for his sons to marry the daughters of the king of Moav?"

Given the hatred Moav felt toward Klal Yisrael, the answer would have to be, "Rich beyond measure."

There is a well-known phrase, "Money marries money." When Rus married Machlon, she was not in any way leaving her life as a princess behind. Marrying the eldest son of the richest Jew in the world meant she could very much anticipate the life that she had become accustomed to living, precisely as she had done before. If there would be any change, it would be that she might expect an even more luxurious existence.

The *Mesillas Yesharim* (ch. 2) quotes Shlomo Hamelech and states, *Whether you become rich or poor, both situations test a Jew's faith* (*Mishlei* 30:9). He then elaborates on the challenges and tests posed by both. The Alshich, though, says that of the two, wealth is the greater *nisayon*. And when it comes as an inheritance, without its possessor having had to work for it (as is usually the case with princes and princesses), that is when money is most toxic and corrupting.

I recall once hearing of a well-known *tzaddekes* who was surrounded by her family on her deathbed, and they asked her for a parting *brachah*. Without hesitation, she said, "You should never be rich!" She did not say they should be poor, of course, but this special lady understood that being rich can be very dangerous.

In English, the phrase "spoiled princess" refers to a girl born into a wealthy family whose *middos* have become twisted and self-centered by the opulent lifestyle in which she was raised. This makes Rus all the more an enigmatic and mysterious character, as her *middos* weren't corrupted at all by the luxury in which she grew up.

Chazal say that the prerequisite to acquiring Torah is *derech eretz*—good character (*Avos* 2:2). Where did this princess, raised her entire life in palaces, used to having people bow down to her and serve her, and now married to a billionaire, possibly acquire *derech eretz*? And Rus's *derech eretz* was not just any *derech eretz,* but the kind that would lead her to embrace the Torah and eventually become the grandmother of Dovid Hamelech and Shlomo Hamelech!

The question goes even deeper.

Chazal refer to Moav as the most despicable of all the nations. As Rav Chaim Friedlander expresses it, *The entire nature of this nation was debauchery* (*Sifsei Chaim, Mo'adim* 3:156). How could anyone overcome an upbringing in a society that embodied the very worst of depravity and reach such stellar heights in the realm of *kedushah*?

Rav Dessler points to the Hebrew word for evil, *ra*, and says that the reverse of "*ra*," spelled *reish ayin*, is "*er*," spelled *ayin reish*. *Er* is the root of the word *hisorerus*, which means a "catalyst" or "awakening." You see *ra* becoming *er* in the lives of Klal Yisrael's *gedolim*. Avraham Avinu had a father who was devoted to the promulgation of idol worship.

Avraham rejected a life of idolatry and became the first to challenge its falsehood. Moshe Rabbeinu was brought up by a man who claimed to be a god. He rejected that lie and went on to refine his character so much that he could stand face-to-face with the real God. Klal Yisrael rejected 210 years of Egyptian corruption and walked away to receive the Torah at Mount Sinai.

By rejecting her society and everything it stood for, Rus became the paradigm of female modesty. She turned *ra* on its head so that it became *er*, the catalyst for her transformation.

Yet still the question remains: What was there deep within this Moabite princess, whose background contained every possible reason for her to become the antithesis of a Jew, to change and embrace *Yiddishkeit*?

The answer is twofold. First, there was her relationship with a *tzaddekes*, Naomi, which anchored her and helped her on her journey. Then, there is a truly amazing insight by the Arizal, which takes us deep into kabbalistic thought: *No Jew ever became an apostate and left the Jewish people, and no non-Jew ever converted and joined Klal Yisrael.*

He is echoing the words of the Ramban, who says the same thing, and Rav Dessler explains what this means:

> There are some Jewish souls that have already been in this world that Heaven has decreed must return [either to repair things they did wrong in a previous life or to achieve what they failed to achieve when they were here]. For some, their *tikkun* will require that they first come into the world as a member of a gentile nation and family. Hashem's kindness allows them to fight their way back to Klal Yisrael and rejoin their actual people so that they are not lost to the Jewish people.
>
> We find converts who after their return went on to become among the very greatest of Klal Yisrael, including renowned *Tanna'im* like Shemayah and Avtalyon. Similarly, we find that the grandsons of Haman taught Torah to the masses (*Sanhedrin* 96b).
>
> (*Haggadah*, p. 34)

The two examples that Rav Dessler cites are, of course, a very brief illustration of the point he is making. The list could have gone on, including Rabbi Akiva, Ben Bag Bag, Ben Hei Hei, and, of course, Onkelos and the prophet Ovadiah, among many more. His explanation that they were actually Jewish souls all along who stumbled in their previous journeys and returned as a consequence leaves an intriguing question hovering in the air. Who were those Jews in those previous journeys? And what did they do wrong that they had to return to repair the damage?

The same intriguing question applies to Rus. In her case, though, the Arizal's *rebbi*, the Alshich Hakadosh, supplies the answer: In her previous life, Rus was the eldest daughter of Lot. Having been sent back to the world as Rus, her journey and its direction was a continuation of one she began long before she was born—or, more accurately, born again. Her actions and the character traits that motivated them as Lot's daughter echoed across time, motivating Rus's actions in her lifetime.

It is hard to see, though, how she did anything wrong and thus required rectification when her soul was first here as Lot's eldest daughter. We already know from the story told by Rav Moshe Feinstein about the man to whom Lot's daughters appeared in a dream that her motivations were completely *l'shem Shamayim*. The name she gave her child made it clear that no child comes into the world except through the union of a man and a woman so that no one could claim that the child was born of a miracle and even establish a false religion around the claim. As we said above, in the merit of exposing themselves to criticism and shame for the good of others and for the sake of Heaven's honor, in the merit of their honesty, the authentic Mashiach would emerge—the very opposite of a false one who would emerge from a lie.

However, for some reason, the soul of Lot's daughter had to return to this world. As explained above, a soul returns to either repair damage the soul caused in a previous existence or to achieve what it failed to achieve in that lifetime. The appearance of Rus tells us that there was still work to do: She was to complete the part she previously played in guaranteeing the arrival of the Mashiach.

Above, we also cited the Midrash, which points to the words that

Lot's eldest daughter chose when she said, *Bring to life seed from our father*, instead of *Bring to life a son from our father* (*Bereishis Rabbah* 51:8). The "seed" to which she was referring and intended to bring into the world was the soul of Mashiach. That was her goal then, and that was her role now. It was for this reason that she returned to this world.

In that case, then, the aspect of "punishment," according to which a Jewish soul has to be born first as a non-Jew and then fight its way back to Klal Yisrael, does not apply to Rus. Why did she have to return in that way?

The answer relates to the theme we have considered several times before. From Yaakov's "inappropriate" expression about his wife to the story of Yehudah and Tamar and all the marriages that contributed to the arrival of Mashiach, they had to camouflage their true motivations and "blindside" the Satan. Nothing could convince him that a marriage could never produce the soul of Mashiach more than a marriage between a rich princess from the despicable nation of Moav to a Jew who stayed outside the land of his people at a time they needed him most.

The life of Rus's spiritual "*alte bubby*" was based on nullifying herself for the sake of others. That *ibergegebenkeit*, that willingness to give of oneself to others, would pass through the generations and embed itself deeply into the spiritual DNA of her granddaughter Rus.

(As an aside, my daughter-in-law is the deputy director of the infertility department of Shaare Zedek Hospital in Yerushalayim. She recently sent me research that shows that people's DNA is affected by their choices and behavior, and those changes are passed on through the generations! Rav Yisrael Salanter actually preempted this study by about two hundred years, when he wrote about this with regard to the mishnah in *Avos* 5:4.)

Rus herself did not marry Machlon to become the spouse of the richest Jew in the world. She married him only after she had undergone *geirus* in order to be part of the family of one of the greatest Jews in the world.

For a Moabite woman, becoming a Jew at that time was problematic. The Torah states that Moabites are barred from joining Klal Yisrael. For decades, there was a question of whether women were also included in the ban. Machlon and Kilyon stood on the side of the debate that women were not included in the ban, and so, Orpah and Rus converted and married them. The question would arise again many times until it would finally be settled during the life of Dovid Hamelech.

The question hung over Dovid's father, Yishai, and threatened his status as a Jew. The Gemara recalls Do'eg raising it again in an attempt to deprive Dovid of the throne and even of his membership in Klal Yisrael (*Yevamos* 76b). When Rus embraced Torah and mitzvos, she knew that there would be many who would refuse to accept her conversion as valid. This was the reason that the man nicknamed Ploni Almoni refused to perform *yibum* and marry her. He believed that since she was a Moabite, he simply couldn't.

Rus was willing to give up her luxurious life and embrace an impoverished one when her husband's fortune disappeared. She subsequently accepted his death and gave up any financial claim she might have had through a *kesubah*, which many would, in any case, see as invalid. Instead, she sat and sewed the shroud in which to bury her dead husband. Then, she followed Naomi to Eretz Yisrael, where she was seen by many as a Moabite, not a Jew. The once fabulously rich princess willingly accepted the ignominy of having to pick up stalks of grain dropped during harvest simply to survive. She did all this so that she could be part of Hashem's people. As she told Naomi, *Your God will be my God…* Nothing would get in the way of her faith.

Rus, after all, had her *bubby's* DNA and her characteristic of ignoring her own feelings of embarrassment for the sake of glorifying Heaven. Rus had the *derech eretz* that must precede Torah, which led her to reject Moav and everything it stood for and accept Torah and mitzvos.

The path of giving up everything that most people consider indispensable is precisely what Klal Yisrael did when they set forth into a desert that could provide them with nothing they needed to survive. As Hashem says, *I recall about you the kindness of your youth, the love you felt toward Me as a bride to her husband, your following Me into the desert, into a land not sown* (*Yirmiyahu* 2:2).

And this is the characteristic that was embedded in Rus that led her to make the choices she did. There was another essential element that

Rus needed in order to fulfill her mission the second time around: Rus was closely connected to a *tzaddekes*, Naomi.

Rav Yitzchak Eizik Sher of Slabodka explains more about how both Rus and her sister Orpah wanted to join Klal Yisrael (*Leket Sichos Mussar*, vol. 2, p. 237). Naomi worked hard to dissuade them, and eventually, Orpah abandoned her dream and returned to her people. Rus stayed tenaciously on her path.

The halachah is clear that if someone wants to convert because they are motivated by a romantic love for a Jew or to gain financial advantage or out of fear of a Jewish army's advance (as they could be killed), the conversion is invalid. But if a non-Jew wants to convert when Jews are experiencing exile and suffering, and his or her motivation is sincere and solely for the sake of Heaven, then the conversion is authentic and valid.

That leaves us with a quandary. Naomi is the name that the Jewish people gave her, according to Rashi. They gave her that name because every aspect of her personality and actions were *na'im*, "pleasant." That is how she came to be known as Naomi, "the pleasant one." It seems clear that Rus's motivation to become a Jew came from her attraction to the charismatic and saintly Naomi. Her own words seem to confirm that: *Only death will separate me from you* (*Rus* 1:17).

This was one of the reasons Naomi tried to dissuade the two sisters from converting. An attachment to the Torah and the Jewish people that is predicated on an attachment to an individual will inevitably fail when the person is no longer there. Rav Zalman Sorotzkin explains that it is for this reason that neither Moshe's birthday nor the day of his death (both were the seventh of Adar) are explicitly mentioned in the Torah. Other religions, *l'havdil*, are built around the life of the founder of that religion. Their founder's birthday and day of death mark the major festivals in their calendar. The Torah didn't want this to apply to Moshe. Klal Yisrael's acceptance and adherence to the Torah are not dependent on us being enthralled with Moshe, and our relationship with him is not the most important relationship for us. That is reserved solely for our relationship with Hashem Himself.

Orpah understood Naomi's message and could easily picture herself at some future time when Naomi was gone. Being a Jew with a Naomi to hold her hand was something any woman would want. She was to her generation what Miriam was to hers. Without that relationship, Orpah's determination evaporated.

With regard to Rus's relationship with Naomi, Rav Yitzchak Eizik Sher goes on to say:

> The relationship that Rus sought with Naomi was not an end in itself, nor was it the cause of her conversion. It was not a relationship she saw as essential. It was rather the means through which she could pursue a relationship with the *Shechinah*... With that, we can come to truly understand Rus, her path, and the difference between her and Orpah.
>
> Orpah was only interested in a relationship with Hashem if her chaperone would be Naomi. Rus understood that as great as the pleasure and beauty was to be had in an attachment to Naomi, it was only a means to an end. The ultimate beauty and pleasure could only be found, as her grandson Dovid Hamelech put it, *As for me? Only closeness to Hashem is good* (Tehillim 73:28).
>
> (*Leket Sichos Mussar*, vol. 2, pp. 239-240)

To reach that goal, Rus understood that she would have to learn from Naomi how to complete her path. She would learn from her how drawing close to Hashem encompasses every single aspect of a Jew's life. It is expressed in the way a Jew walks or sleeps. It is reinforced by the people they walk beside on their journey and by how they eventually return their soul to the place where it originated.

Rus expressed this to Naomi with the words, *Do not pressure me to abandon you and leave you. Where you walk, I will walk; where you sleep, I will sleep; and your people shall be my people. The way you die will be the way that I die, too* (Rus 1:16-17).

At that point, Naomi abandoned her attempts to dissuade Rus. She heard in her words that she didn't simply have an outstanding daughter-in-law. She had an outstanding *talmidah*.

Secure in that knowledge, Naomi could now demand of Rus something that went against her very nature but would secure the onward path of Mashiach. She would ask Rus to go to Boaz's tent in a way that would be perfectly natural for a *bas Moav* but abhorrent to a *bas Yisrael*. She knew that Rus understood that, *If your* rav *tells you your right hand is your left hand and your left hand is your right one, you should still listen to him* (*Devarim* 17:11 and *Sifri* there).

And so, on the night that the harvest concluded, Rus went to Boaz and started the chain of events where the "seed" she spoke about as Lot's daughter, the seed of Mashiach, would grow within her and produce a great-grandson called Dovid.

The Gemara adds a beautiful and moving epilogue to the story of Rus (*Bava Basra* 91b).

When her great-grandson Shlomo Hamelech sat on his throne (which was constructed to echo mystical concepts of the Torah), there was a smaller throne beside his, where his great-grandmother, Rus, sat. It is unusual for a person to see the fruits of their *mesirus nefesh* for Hashem and Klal Yisrael during their own lifetime. As *Chazal* put it, no one leaves this world with even half of what they want to achieve fulfilled (*Koheles Rabbah* 1:13). The story of Rus is an exception to that rule. She saw Klal Yisrael at its greatest. She saw the Beis Hamikdash being built, started by her grandson Dovid and completed by his son Shlomo. Rus was one of the few people in history who were shown a little of the reward that awaited her in return for her determination to become part of the Jewish people. Despite Naomi's attempts to dissuade her, she would not be turned away and declared, *Your people will be my people!*

CHAPTER TWENTY-FIVE

Mrs. Caroline Pakter

I OFTEN TRAVEL TO Edgware in London to speak in a shul called Adas Yisrael. The *rav*, Rabbi Tzvi Hirsch Lieberman, is a good friend, and two of my *talmidim* organize the trip. The most enjoyable part of speaking is the large number of people who come over to recall that I taught them ten, twenty, or thirty years ago.

On the way back from shul a few years ago, I bumped into a young lady and her husband walking along with their children. Her face broke into a smile when she saw me. The hands of the clock of my memory spun backward eighteen years.

"Do you remember," she asked her children, "that Mummy told you that she wasn't always *frum?*"

The little faces looking at her nodded, and she pointed to me.

"Well, you see this rabbi? I used to go to his *shiur* every week!" Then, she looked at me, pointed to her beautiful children, and said, "This is where those *shiurim* led."

Caroline Pakter was born in Edgware, where her family attended a Reform synagogue. Her father was a successful accountant, and her mother looked after her two young daughters and was involved in cancer care.

From an early age, Caroline's great loves were dance and music. Her great-aunt was a well-known opera singer in Los Angeles, and Caroline herself was blessed with an astonishingly beautiful voice.

She attended one of London's most prestigious schools, Haberdashers' Aske's School for Girls. Singing and music continued to be essential to the talented young lady, but she also had a natural affinity for languages, and so, she went on to the University of Birmingham to study French and Spanish. During her first year, she discovered that there was a competition to find the "Jewish Performer of the Year" held in the prestigious London Palladium Theater. Caroline auditioned and won second place. One of the judges spotted her talent, and upon hearing that she was studying languages, persuaded her to change direction and apply to the Liverpool Institute of Performing Arts (LIPA).

I used to visit Liverpool every Wednesday and give a *shiur* to Jewish university students. That was where I first met the young woman then called Caroline Cohen.

Moving to Liverpool made Caroline feel a certain longing for the Friday-night meals that her family, though not religious, still kept as she grew up. But her childhood Friday-night meals were more cultural events than spiritual ones, with the TV playing in the background as the family sat around the table with the flickering candles to eat Jewish food.

At her first Shabbos meal in Liverpool, there was no TV flickering in the corner. Instead, there was the melody of Jewish *zemiros*, and for the young woman whose first love was music and singing, she was enraptured.

The next toe she dipped into the waters of *Yiddishkeit* was accepting an invitation to eat in the home of the local Chabad rabbi, who added a warm family element to the picture that was starting to come into focus for her—a picture of what a true Shabbos could be. Caroline now had a second love to add to her first one, and since it contained so much music, Shabbos soon became an essential part of who she was.

Her next great leap forward was to join an Aish trip to Eretz Yisrael. Shabbos, *zemiros*, and *divrei Torah* were now set against the backdrop of the golden stones of Yerushalayim and the Kosel. Caroline's picture was now complete, and it led her to a crisis.

There were two paths lying before her, and they could not have been more different. The white and gold stones of Yerushalayim and a life of *shemiras hamitzvos* lay on one side, and the tinsel and rhinestones that a life in the theater had to offer were waiting for her on the other.

The choice is not as clear and obvious as it appears.

I have always wondered about those who had everything *Olam Hazeh* could possibly offer, like Basya the daughter of Pharaoh, Rus, and Yisro and his daughters, and yet they gave it all up to embrace Torah and mitzvos. In my lifetime, I have met quite a few special young people who had glittering futures awaiting them, and yet, they abandoned that life and chose Torah instead. And don't forget—the Satan is a "wise old king" who knows exactly how to make what he is offering appear every bit as appealing as the alternative.

In her final year at LIPA, Caroline watched as her friends sent off their resumes to theatrical agents who could open the doors they so sought, but she hesitated. Her childhood dream of performing on stage beckoned, but the music of Shabbos, so recently discovered, pulled her, too.

Then the Satan revealed his masterstroke.

One of Caroline's fellow students had managed to sign a contract with the UK's leading agent for musical theater. He confided in his new "star" that he had tried and failed to find an understudy for one of the most famous theatrical roles of all in a show called *My Fair Lady*. The student immediately recommended her friend with the astonishingly beautiful voice.

Amazingly, instead of issuing a summons to come and audition for him, he traveled to Liverpool to listen to her there. It was like magic! (The Satan is good at "magic.") Without even applying for the part, Caroline now had the sort of start the people in her school dreamed of. From that came other auditions and roles as London's theater world, the "West End," learned of the remarkably talented young star.

Being torn between two worlds is not a comfortable situation to find yourself in. Just to make sure that there wasn't the slightest possibility that Caroline would allow her new love—Shabbos—to replace her old love, the Satan produced his final stroke of genius.

There was one part in a certain musical that Caroline had dreamed of above all others. Her agent called her to explain that she was to audition for the lead in this coveted role. And then, something strange happened.

The audition was around Shavuos time, and as she sat in the taxi that would take her from the religious area where she lived, Golders Green, to that other world of fame and celebrity, she turned around in the taxi to look back and suddenly knew that she didn't want to go.

Instead of winning a role that would have brought her everything that *Olam Hazeh* and the Satan could possibly offer, she went home and had her Shavuos meal with another rabbi who had been influential in her life, Rabbi Akiva Tatz. Caroline finally knew that this "stage"— set with flickering candles instead of glaring stage lights, and laughing children instead of clapping strangers, enhanced by Jewish music that touched her soul—was where she truly belonged.

Caroline took her "show on the road" and went back to the golden stones of Yerushalayim. There, she attended Neve Yerushalayim seminary for *ba'alei teshuvah*. Shortly afterward, she met her husband, Grant, who was learning at Ohr Somayach, and they married. Soon, the first of the children she introduced me to came along.

Today, Caroline takes her talent, her beautiful voice, and her story around the world in a truly inspirational show for Jewish women. And for women who have always wondered, as I did, about people to whom the Satan offered everything and who turned him down, I'll give you a "*heter*" to spend a night at the theater and see a show called *From Showbiz to Shabbos*.

CHAPTER TWENTY-SIX

Nitzeves: Molding Hashem's Masterpiece

THE LIFE OF Dovid Hamelech, the major challenges and drama-filled incidents along his path to the throne, is well known. The drama and challenges his mother faced are less well known. In fact, I have always been surprised how few people actually even know that her name was Nitzeves bas Ada'el.

One of the most famous stories in Tanach is the crowning of Dovid as Shaul Hamelech's successor. It is also one of the major episodes on Dovid Hamelech's path and that of his future descendant, Mashiach.

The prophet Shmuel was considered equal to Moshe and Aharon combined. Hashem told him to go to the house of Yishai, and that was where he would find and anoint the next king of Klal Yisrael. Yishai, Dovid's father, was the greatest rabbi of his generation. The Gemara (*Yevamos* 76b) reports that when he traveled from his home, he was accompanied by 600,000 people. When Shmuel explained to Yishai why he had come, he promptly gathered his seven sons and presented them to the *Navi*. As soon as he set eyes on Yishai's eldest son, Eliav, Shmuel was convinced that he had found the man he had been sent to anoint. Immediately, Hashem spoke to him and contradicted his conclusion.

Hashem used words that hold as much relevance and wisdom today as they did then:

> Do not look at his appearance or his physical stature, for I have rejected him. It is not as man sees, [only what is visible] to the eyes, but Hashem sees into the heart.
>
> (*Shmuel I* 16:7)

Dovid's heart was clearly different from those of his brothers, but his physical appearance, too, was dissimilar to theirs, and that fact would play a crucial part in his story and the greatness he achieved.

Ultimately, the architect who carefully crafted his journey was his mother, Nitzeves. To understand her story, we have to examine another well-known story along the path on the journey to Mashiach.

At the time that this story unfolds, the Jewish nation was at war with the Philistines, and the two armies met each other across a field. A common feature of the battles of the ancient world, both armies' champions would challenge each other to single combat.

As in any game with high rewards, the risks were high, too. If your champion won, it would inspire and give confidence to his fellow soldiers and dishearten the enemy. The danger was that if he lost, it would have the opposite effect.

The Philistines had a champion who could not fail to win. His name was Golias, and he was over twelve feet tall. The Jewish army was terrified of this giant, and Shaul Hamelech realized that unless he could find someone who would answer the challenge, the enemy had already won the psychological advantage—and the war. He offered rich rewards, including his daughter's hand in marriage, to any man who would pick up the gauntlet Golias had thrown down.

When Shaul saw Dovid running toward Golias, he turned to his general, Avner, and asked a puzzling question: *The son of whom is this lad, Avner?* The general gave an equally baffling reply: *By your life, O King, I do not know!* (*Shmuel I* 17:55).

This exchange between the general and his king can only leave the reader confused. We already know that Dovid's father was the greatest rabbi of his time. Dovid was extremely close to Shaul and even carried his armor. How could he suddenly feign ignorance about who Dovid was and where he came from?

The Gemara explains that Shaul was actually asking Avner a very different question, and that was the reason he had no answer (*Yevamos* 76b). As Rashi points out, the offer of Shaul's daughter in marriage could mean that Dovid would be a potential rival to the throne over the king's son, Yonasan. That threat was only possible if he was a direct descendant of Yehudah through his son Peretz, but not if he had descended from Yehudah's other son, Zerach. That was the answer Shaul was seeking from Avner. And Peretz was indeed Dovid's ancestor.

The conversation between the king and his general triggered an intervention from the head of Shaul's *beis din*, Do'eg Ha'Edomi. Do'eg scoffed at the debate about Dovid's lineage and his worthiness to become a king, saying that first, Shaul should inquire whether Dovid was even fit to be a member of the Jewish people! Do'eg pointed to the fact that Dovid was a direct descendant of Rus and consequently insisted that Dovid therefore could not be part of the Jewish nation, let alone its royal family.

According to the halachah, though, a Moabitess convert is accepted into the Jewish people. It is only male Moabite converts who are forbidden to marry Jews by birth. This distinction was not generally understood or accepted by the Jewish people at that time, though the ruling had been formulated by the Sanhedrin in the time of Boaz and by Shmuel and his *beis din*.

This was not the first time that Dovid's status had been challenged. The first time was by his own father, who was the greatest rabbi of his time.

Yishai is one of those people who is named as someone who lived and died without once sinning (*Rashi, Sanhedrin* 77a). Yishai was a uniquely holy human being, and he believed that Dovid was not his son at all. Yishai believed that Dovid was a *mamzer*!

How did this come about?

Toward the end of Yishai's life, the old controversy about whether a Moabitess could enter the Jewish people flared up again. Yishai himself wasn't sure what the true Torah position in the matter was. That was something that was only going to be settled in the aftermath of Dovid's victory over Golias. In the meantime, Yishai now had doubts about his legitimacy as part of the Jewish nation.

He already had seven sons from his wife, Nitzeves. If the halachah was ruled against him, that would mean that as a grandson of Rus, he was not a part of the Jewish people, and neither were his seven sons. Any other children born to him through his wife would face the same stigma and rejection. Yishai devised an ingenious solution: He would separate from his wife and instead take her *shifchah*, her maidservant, as a wife.

A *shifchah* is a non-Jewish maidservant who has undertaken to keep the Torah's laws upon becoming part of a Jewish family. It is, in effect, a partial conversion; though she kept those laws, she was considered a non-Jew while she remained a maidservant. Yishai's solution was to marry her based on a halachic technicality. If his grandmother Rus was a halachically valid convert who was able to join the Jewish people, Yishai was a full Jew unrestricted by any marital limitations. He was therefore freeing his wife's maidservant based on that assumption. The act of freeing her would automatically bestow on her *full* Jewish status, and she would leave her *shifchah* status behind and become a Jew. If she were a full convert, there was no reason he could not marry her, and there would be no questions regarding any children she would bear him. They, too, would be fully Jewish.

The second part of his strategy rested on the possibility of him *not* being a full member of the Jewish people. If that was the case, he would intend that his act of freeing her would have no legal force. As someone forbidden to marry a woman who was born Jewish, like Nitzeves, he would be able to marry a *shifchah*, something prohibited to a full member of Klal Yisrael.

Either way, he saw this as a neat solution. Yishai preferred any new children who would be born to him to be the sons of a *shifchah*, and they would therefore be *avadim*, the male equivalent. Subsequently, they could be freed and would emerge as full Jews.

This was the crucial element of Yishai's plan—that they would emerge as full Jews in their own right. A convert is halachically viewed as reborn, which means that their connection to their biological father would be severed. The Moabite ban that affected him would not affect them, and they could go on to marry into the Jewish people.

The Rama MiPano takes up the story and explains what happened when Yishai put his plan into effect:

> The woman he planned to marry was Nitzeves's maid-servant. She was loyal to her mistress, and she believed that the halachah indicated that a Moabitess was permitted to convert and marry into the Jewish people without hindrance. This meant that Yishai's three-year separation from his wife was unnecessary and wrong.
>
> She decided to employ the strategy of Rachel and Leah. She told her mistress exactly what she should say to convince Yishai that she was the maidservant. She extinguished the candles before he came to her room on their wedding night, and the two women exchanged roles.
>
> The plot worked perfectly, and Nitzeves conceived a child. In the morning she left before dawn, and her maidservant slipped inside the room to take her place. Yishai awoke to find his new wife exactly where he expected her to be. He was totally unaware that he had spent the night with his old wife.
>
> Neither told him what they had done.

Months later, when it became known that Nitzeves, his estranged wife, was pregnant, he and their sons were convinced that she had committed adultery. What other explanation was possible? When the child was born, it was a boy, and unlike her other sons, he was red-haired and small. His appearance added supplementary evidence to the accusation that this child was a *mamzer*. It was a disgrace that Yishai and his sons concealed: Yishai made him a shepherd, a job that would keep him separate and removed from his brothers and the rest of his family.

Shmuel's question to Yishai many years later, *Don't you have any other sons?* pointed to the extent to which Dovid's father and brothers had rejected him. It also tells us, as Rav Chaim Friedlander says in his *sefer Sifsei Chaim*, that he was sincere when he only brought Dovid's seven brothers before Shmuel to be selected as king. Shmuel had asked for all his sons. Yishai believed that Dovid was not his son.

But Nitzeves's actions emulated more than one mother of Klal Yisrael. In never revealing to her husband who Dovid's father was, she also copied the actions of Tamar and her behavior toward Yehudah. Like Tamar, Nitzeves, too, remained silent—in part, to avoid embarrassing Yishai when he would realize that he had been tricked into conceiving another son with her.

She had an additional and even greater reason for keeping her secret, and it becomes apparent when we consider the very different outcomes between the episode with Tamar and the one with Nitzeves.

Tamar's actions ended the accusation against her immediately, and neither of her sons suffered as a consequence of what she did. Nitzeves's long silence would condemn Dovid to a childhood and early manhood of insult and rejection. Her silence and her son's resulting banishment as a shepherd guarding his flock from danger could have ended his life: Both a bear and a lion tried to kill him in his role as shepherd. The obvious question is: Why didn't she share the truth of Dovid's origin with her husband and save Dovid all that pain and suffering?

We can start to answer this question by considering the words of Rav Yosef Salant in his *sefer Be'er Yosef*. He quotes the midrash regarding the *pasuk*, *Every word of Hashem is perfect; He is a shield to those who trust in Him* (*Mishlei* 30:5) and states:

> Hashem does not give greatness to an individual until he has been tested in small matters, and only then is he elevated to greatness. There are two examples of the greatest of Klal Yisrael whom Hashem tested first in small matters, found them reliable, and only then promoted them to bigger things. Dovid was tested first as a shepherd, when he only grazed the sheep in the desert to make sure they didn't eat in fields that did not belong to him... Hashem said, "I have found you reliable with your flocks. Now come and shepherd Mine." The same was true of Moshe.

This midrash seems strange. Surely if someone is capable of great things, you can conclude that he would easily be able to perform well when it comes to small and simple matters. The logic does not work the other way around.

Imagine your nine-year-old son came to proudly show you that he had successfully reattached a wire that had come loose in his toy car so that its lights would work again. Would it make sense for you to express your happiness and pride and then tell him, "Well, son, as you clearly have a talent in this field, I would like you to rewire the entire house tomorrow"?

The *Be'er Yosef* explains that the midrash is conveying a different idea entirely:

> Both Moshe and Dovid had already proven themselves with great deeds before they became the leaders of Klal Yisrael. Moshe was already called an *ish haElokim*, "a man of God," and Dovid was already the composer of Tehillim, *a brilliant and fearless soldier, immensely wise, and handsome, and Hashem was with him* (*Shmuel* I 16:18).
>
> Yet despite their greatness, they were still able to "come down" to the level of ordinary "small" people and their mundane, everyday concerns.
>
> This is very difficult for geniuses who occupy the highest spiritual heights to do. For such people, the world and its concerns are irrelevant... That is why they have to be tested before Hashem appoints them to leadership roles: It is to make sure that they still understand the minds and concerns of ordinary people.
>
> This is the reason why the Midrash reports that Moshe ran after a lamb who had become lost and carried it back on his shoulders. It is why Dovid made sure that the young sheep were able to graze first and ate the tender grass, aware that their immature teeth could eat only the soft grass. He made sure to leave the tough grass for the older sheep with fully developed teeth that could comfortably eat it.

The greater the role that Hashem requires a Jew to occupy, the more the Jew needs to experience a rigorous apprenticeship to qualify him or her for the position. You would hardly expect that someone who came from a background of privilege, brought up as an Egyptian prince, would show any empathy for slaves. Yet not only did Moshe go out to see his brothers in their enslavement, but he also worked alongside them, pulling huge stones and shouldering their burden.

Similarly, you would hardly expect someone who was scorned by all and despised as a *mamzer* to become the king of the Jewish people. But the truth is that it is particularly those who face numerous challenges and overcome them who have a better chance of achieving greatness.

This was apparent in the life of Yaakov Avinu, as we discussed above. Before his confrontation with Esav, Yaakov sent a message to Esav saying, Garti *(I have dwelled) with Lavan.* Rashi points out that the word *garti* is spelled with the same letters as *taryag*, 613. In this way, Yaakov was hinting that he had not been corrupted by living all those years with his crooked father-in-law and still adhered to all 613 mitzvos of the Torah.

Rav Yerucham Levovitz understands Yaakov's message differently: It was specifically *because* he lived with such a corrupt individual, who cheated and swindled him countless times, that he was able to keep the 613 mitzvos.

Sometimes, it is only lives with the harshest of beginnings that can deliver the greatest conclusions!

The same idea is expressed in the *pasuk* in which Shlomo Hamelech wrote, *The crucible is for silver and the furnace for gold, and a man according to his praise (Mishlei 27:21).* According to the Ibn Ezra, "his praise" refers to a man's willingness to allow himself to accept events that could purify him and consciously let go of his impurities.

The gold may have to enter the flames many times to become completely pure. Likewise, Dovid would have to endure much to achieve the complete purification that would allow him to fulfill his reason for being in this world—to be the king of Bnei Yisrael.

Rav Dessler writes about another Jew Hashem would promote to greatness: Yosef Hatzaddik.

> It is intriguing that when Yosef reveals himself to his brothers, he tells them, "I am Yosef, whom you sold to Egypt." Then he says, "Do not be distressed and do not let it

trouble you that you sold me here, for it was to preserve life that God sent me before you."

Then he continues, "Now realize that it was not you who sent me here but God, and He made me a father to Pharaoh, a lord over all his household, and a ruler over the entire land of Egypt."

Yosef's rulership of Egypt was solely a gift from Hashem. It was the essential element that allowed him to weaken Egypt's ability to destroy the Jewish people during the imminent exile. To be worthy of that role, Yosef would have to endure the most difficult of tests. He would be sold as a slave. Those who sold him would be his own brothers, magnifying his pain. The place where he was made a slave would be the one that treated its slaves worse than any other—Egypt. It was a place where escape was a complete impossibility.

Then, a glimmer of light appeared at the end of a dark tunnel: His master noticed his talents and gifts and promoted him. But subsequently, the truly dreadful test with Potifar's wife threatened to engulf him. He passed the test but was still accused of wrongdoing. He was tried, convicted, and thrown in jail.

Through all this, he never once questioned the justice and rightness of the chain of events Hashem had orchestrated for him. Yosef accepted it all with love.

This awful set of circumstances with one crushing blow after another produced an ordeal that Yosef would endure and conquer. His unwavering *bitachon* and unquestioning certainty in Hashem's love for him would eventually produce the series of miracles that would make him ruler of Egypt.

There was no moment of self-pity, no question of "Why me?"

(*Michtav Me'Eliyahu*, vol. 2, p. 232)

Self-pity would have been understandable from someone who had been rejected by his father and brothers. It would have been natural from someone whom everyone shunned for being a *mamzer* and was left to shepherd alone at the risk of death. Instead, it produced someone whose songs of love and connection between a Jew and his Maker have been an inspiration to Klal Yisrael since the moment they were written.

But what of his mother, who stood back, watching her son's suffering? Why didn't she act to end it?

The spiritual level of Dovid's father was so high that he is repeatedly mentioned by *Chazal* as dying only as the sole consequence of Adam Harishon's sin, which condemned everyone to die. If not for that, he would have lived forever, having never sinned himself (*Yevamos* 77a).

Therefore, we need to reevaluate his relationship with and treatment of his son. But let us set that aside for now and consider what sort of woman this unique human being who never sinned chose as a wife.

It's obvious that Yishai chose a woman who was on a spiritual level that matched his own. Rav Yitzchak Hutner says precisely that in his *sefer Pachad Yitzchak*: *There is a* segulah *in saying the name of Nitzeves bas Ada'el seventeen times before praying to Heaven* (vol. 4, p. 87).

The Chida states:

> Nitzeves bas Ada'el was a complete saint. It pained her immensely when her husband separated from her. The belief of Yishai and his sons that their mother had committed adultery and that Dovid was the outcome of that crime was part of the ongoing process of hiding the path that would lead to Mashiach.
>
> Dovid was the "black sheep of the family" and was indeed distanced and isolated from it by being a shepherd. People assumed that he was forced into isolation because he had done something very wrong in his father's home to have deserved such rejection, and they too shunned him.
>
> All this followed the pattern of hiding Mashiach and his journey from the Satan, who would have exerted the greatest efforts to disrupt that journey.
>
> This was to be the last and greatest concealment before Dovid Hamelech's ascension to the throne and the establishment of his line, which would culminate in the arrival of Mashiach. This concealment was even hidden from his

father, his brothers, and every other Jew in his time, including even Shmuel Hanavi, who was considered to be the equivalent of Moshe and Aharon combined (in terms of his prophetic ability), until Hashem tore away the veil and commanded Shmuel to, *Rise up and anoint him as king, for he is the one!*

It is intriguing to note that the Chida states that Dovid's journey was hidden from his father but does not say that it was hidden from his *mother*.

We noted earlier that the Alshich makes an intriguing point when he discusses another key female figure who crafted part of Mashiach's path, Naomi:

> Naomi was a woman who was exceptional in saintliness. It was this fact that caused Rus to go against her every instinct as a Jew and obey her instruction to go to Boaz. Had Rus not had confidence in Naomi's merit, she would not have obeyed… But it was not just that Naomi had reached the pinnacle of refinement as a human being. She also possessed *ruach hakodesh*!
>
> It was not hidden from Naomi that a unique soul would emerge from Moav. This soul would be the result of the actions of Lot's daughter, who acted solely for the sake of Heaven, fully conscious that she would be bringing the soul of Mashiach into the world by her actions.

Would it be hard to imagine that the woman who was the perfect match of a man who lived an entire lifetime without sinning once, who was, as the Chida states, *a complete saint*, knew all this, too? It's easy to believe that Nitzeves knew that Mashiach needed to emerge from Moav. She certainly knew about her husband's lineage before she married him. She also knew that he was a complete tzaddik who came from the messianic line. We will soon see that she also possessed *ruach hakodesh*.

As we said before, Nitzeves knew all this, and she also knew that with a few words, she could end Dovid's isolation and pain by revealing to Yishai that Dovid was his son. Yet, she didn't say anything, and

Dovid suffered. As the *sefer Kol Tzofiach* says, *Dovid Hamelech was born into a life of suffering. From the day of his birth he bore pain, and despite the amount and intensity of that pain, he accepted it with love for Hashem.*

But Nitzeves did nothing to relieve him of this pain. That's because it was necessary. As Rav Chaim Friedlander explains:

> The twenty-eight years of Dovid's rejection by his father and his brothers was all to prepare him for kingship. When someone comes from a distinguished background and faces rejection and humiliation, it usually drives him to display his gifts and talents in order to prove how great he is. In the case of Dovid, the opposite occurred. He did not see their rejection as diminishing who and what he was in the slightest. He did not feel the need to show them that they were wrong. The converse was true: Dovid continued working on his trait of humility.
>
> Even after he was anointed, and all the pieces of the puzzle of his life were fit into place, he remained unchanged. A lesser man might have lorded it over others, particularly those who had done so much to diminish him throughout his life. Dovid bore the process of his anointment and elevation to kingship without it changing him in the slightest. Immediately after the ceremony, he returned to his flock and his role as a shepherd.
>
> *(Middos V'Avodas Hashem, p. 207)*

Nitzeves watched every part of her son's rejection up until the arrival of Shmuel to anoint him. She also understood that it was all necessary to ready her son to be the anointed king. She therefore could not interrupt it to mitigate Dovid's suffering. That suffering's climax was the crucial process that imprinted the essential ingredient on every aspect of his being: humility. This is the *middah* that would lead Mashiach to his throne.

She also knew that in keeping the truth of her story secret, the Satan would pose no threat to him or suspect him of being Mashiach. Why would this wretched and rejected boy require his special efforts to sabotage his journey?

Thus, we find that the Midrash teaches:

> Shmuel stood and anointed Dovid... At that moment, his mother said, *Even ma'asu habanim hayesah l'rosh pinah*—"The stone that the builders rejected became the cornerstone of the Temple" (*Tehillim* 118:22). Nitzeves was implying, "*Ei ben*—who is the son—who was rejected by the *banim*, the sons?" He is the one who became the foundation and superior to all of them.
>
> (*Yalkut Mechiri, Tehillim* 118)

And so, there is clear evidence that Nitzeves had *ruach hakodesh*, the same *ruach hakodesh* that inspired Dovid to choose the words that formed *sefer Tehillim*.

His brothers, too, were blessed with the phenomenon of *ruach hakodesh*, as they added their own words that would be incorporated into Dovid's *Tehillim*: *This came from Hashem!... This is the day that Hashem made. Rejoice and be happy in it!* (*Tehillim* 118:23–24). Nitzeves's sons, Dovid's brothers, now understood that their accusation against their mother and Dovid was false, and they declared their happiness and joy at being able to see how Hashem's hand had orchestrated the entire situation through the actions of their mother, who had fashioned someone who would be Hashem's masterpiece, *Dovid melech Yisrael*.

CHAPTER TWENTY-SEVEN

Mrs. Rachely Plancey

O N THURSDAY, JANUARY 25, 2018, I left JFK Airport for the most unusual trip I'd ever taken. The first odd thing I encountered was that although Delta's website told me that every seat on the plane was taken, it turned out that they weren't. In fact, the two next to mine were completely empty, allowing me to stretch out and transform an economy-class seat into a first-class one. And when I arrived at Heathrow Airport, I was a half hour early. I got through customs in an instant, and my bag was second off the conveyor belt.

I fly a lot. These things don't happen.

I went outside to await the arrival of the shuttle that would take me from the airport terminal to the car rental company. The car was already parked there, waiting for me. Since I was the only pickup, I had soon filled out the paperwork, refused the offer of an upgrade to a Mercedes for "very little money," and was driving away in a Mini Cooper.

I was in England to speak at one of Camp Simcha UK's family weekend retreats. The founders of Camp Simcha UK are Meir Plancey and his wife, Rachely. If you want to see what a warm smile looks like, you have to meet Meir. If you want to see two such smiles, you have to meet him with his wife, Rachely. Meir's father is a *rav* in Glasgow, Scotland, but he was brought up in London and learned at Sunderland

Yeshivah and Midrash Shmuel under the *rosh yeshivah* and tzaddik, Rav Binyomin Moskowitz. Rachely was also born in London, as was her father. Her mother was born in Antwerp and brought up in Israel.

I met the Planceys for the first time at that weekend, an annual Shabbaton they run for children with serious conditions and diseases other than cancer. I wanted to know what led Meir to start an organization whose work is nothing short of astonishing and, indeed, holy. Such organizations are usually started by people who themselves have sick children. Meir wasn't even married when he started working with the children.

"Well," he explained, "I was brought up in a *rav's* home. I suppose helping people is in my blood."

While he was learning at Midrash Shmuel in Yerushalayim, he was boarding with a family whose five-year-old son developed a brain tumor. Meir witnessed the toll the aggressive chemotherapy had on the child, and this gave him an insight. There was nothing he could do about the effects of the treatment, but he could do something about the times when the child wasn't having treatment.

Meir began reading stories to the little boy, and then his inventive mind conjured games and a score of other distractions. His goal was to give the boy enough joyful experiences and memories so that when he looked back he'd remember the happy times and forget about the other ones. He also often accompanied the boy to the hospital to offer support to his young friend.

In 1994, Meir's time in full-time learning drew to a close, and he wondered if he could bring his approach in helping sick children back to help families in the UK. With three volunteers, he did just that.

Meir started a professional career as a financial adviser and became engaged to Rachely. The couple had a discussion about Meir's activities helping really sick children. Was it time, he wondered, to step back and concentrate on building his own family? Or should they take the fledgling organization to the next step and make it grow?

If you know Meir, you'll know that the choice was clear. In any case, Rachely was quite certain: She was marrying Meir *and* all his sick kids, too.

Even during the couple's *sheva brachos* week, they were planning Rachely's first dramatic induction into the world that would become her life. They were about to take five children with cancer to the United States to join Camp Simcha UK's summer camp. The planning for such a venture, which included bringing a nurse with them to care for the children, was extremely complicated, but Rachely took it all in stride.

I asked her if she had any background in caring for very sick children when she undertook to build a family that would be busier than most. She replied that she had no experience in this field at all, but she conceded that she had always been involved in helping people who were in trouble or needed a little more support in life.

In 1995, Camp Simcha UK became an official charity operating out of the new Plancey family house in London's Golders Green. Volunteers appeared in large numbers to meet the growing demand. Meir told me that his view was that if someone else was helping sick children better than he was, Camp Simcha UK would back off and let them. Meir and Rachely are allergic to politics, especially if it interferes with their ability to maximize the help offered to people who need it.

In June 2009, the charity moved into its first real office, and by then, the Planceys had been blessed with four children. Rachely emphasized to me that her children and husband always come first.

When the family was still small, with just two children, they would bring the children to the weekend retreats for couples with sick children. When their eldest turned six, she decided that this was no longer possible. Her children might recognize some of the families, and one of her greatest concerns has always been guarding her clients' confidentiality. This is where Rachely's mother, who lives only two doors away, stepped in. The children would spend the weekend with her whenever their parents were hosting Shabbatons for the sick children and their parents.

"My mother was my backbone," Rachely told me. "I could never have juggled both roles without her support."

Rachely's main role in the organization was family liaison officer. That role involved her going to meet the parents of sick children to assess their needs—the needs *they* felt they had. It was not her job, she explained, to tell them what help they should accept but discover what help they were comfortable accepting.

Today, her team includes fourteen family liaison officers, offering clients twenty-five different services from transportation to and from the hospital to financial aid. When I asked her how she deals with the terrible pain and suffering, she offered an intriguing response:

"You have to maintain a professional distance from the people you are helping. Otherwise, you simply would not be able to do the best job on their behalf. But I think we do a bit more. In fact, when I interview people to do this work, if I feel they will not be affected by the work at all, then they are not the right person for the job."

At the Camp Simcha UK retreat that I attended, I watched at the Friday-night meal as one of the organization's favorite attendees, Rabbi Fachler, was busy using his superb sense of humor to bring laughter to the hundred or so parents, their children, and the volunteers. Standing at one of the tables, a mother was holding a bottle filled with a white liquid high in the air. She looked like a real-life Statue of Liberty. A tube led from the bottle straight into her nine-year-old child's stomach. This was how he "ate." The child's attention was totally focused on Rabbi Fachler and the joy he brought to the hundreds of people in the room. No one stared at the mother and her child or at any of the other children. Everyone was too busy having a great time.

I was scheduled to speak three times that Shabbos, but the mothers attending with their children asked for an additional *shmuess*. After Shabbos, several of the parents wanted to meet with me and discuss their situations. There were fourteen couples seeking meetings and simply not enough time for them all. But that was not a problem for Rachely Plancey. She announced that that the sessions had to be limited to a strict twenty minutes each to make sure that everyone had a chance to tell their tales and ask their questions. She stood outside the door to monitor the sessions and make sure couples were sticking to the rules and everyone had a chance.

I listened to stories of the challenges posed by a sick child's siblings who felt neglected as their mother and father rushed from one crisis or hospital appointment to another and another. I learned about the strains on their marriages or their finances (serious illness, even in the UK with its free National Health Service, is still the biggest thief of all). I heard many other worries and fears that night. And I heard all of that from some of the bravest and most devoted parents I have ever met.

At a subsequent Shabbaton, the siblings of the Camp Simcha UK children asked for their own sessions. Mrs. Plancey arranged for me to give the talks for sisters and brothers, too. Afterward, she suggested that I send them a monthly *chizuk* video message.

A few years ago, a gala dinner was held to mark the twentieth anniversary of Camp Simcha UK. It had traveled a long way from its humble beginnings of taking five sick children to the United States for a break. The organization now has a £2 million annual budget, a large staff, and an ever-growing number of families seeking their help.

There was a surprise awaiting the Planceys at that dinner. The Camp Simcha UK staff had produced a book about all the families Meir and Rachely had helped over the past twenty years. It contained messages and blessings from them all to the couple who had seen their suffering and knew how to assess their needs and offer the help *they* felt they needed.

They wanted the book to be presented by a member of the family Meir had boarded with in Yerushalayim as a *bachur* so many years ago, whose son had inspired all of Meir and Rachely's life work.

The family was flown in from Eretz Yisrael, and the story of Meir's "first family" was told to the large gathering. All eyes then turned to the special guests from Eretz Yisrael who would be presenting to the Planceys the amazing book that the staff had produced.

A young man stood up with the book in his hand and began to walk toward the Planceys' table. Meir had first known him as a little five-year-old with an aggressive brain tumor. That little boy, now twenty-five years old, wanted to express his thanks, and that of so many others, to his old friend.

I was not at that special event, but I am confident that there was not a dry eye in the room at that presentation. I am wiping tears from my own eyes just writing about it now.

I once asked Meir, "What is your warmest memory, out of the twenty-five years in which you and your wife went from personally helping a few children, to employing fourteen family liaison officers who deliver 8,500 hours of care per year to 1,000 family members?"

He told me, "Many of our children who survived cancer went on to enter the medical profession, so some of the doctors who come to our retreats to help our very sick children were very sick children themselves not too long ago. Seeing how far they've come gives me the most satisfaction."

Rachely answered the same question by painting the picture for me that came into her mind when I asked it:

It has always been a source of real satisfaction to her that the organization she and her husband created has been there for every kind of Jew, from the most religious to Jews who barely know that they are Jewish.

She recalled at one of her Shabbatons watching two mothers sitting together on the lawn of a hotel watching their children. One of their little girls ran around laughing in the sunshine with her newly regrown hair streaming behind her. Both mothers had traveled the terrible and dark journey of having a very sick child and, despite their different religious levels, sat as friends. Both were enjoying the fact that, with more than a little help from Meir and Rachely Plancey, they had come through their dark times to watch a little girl laughing, running, and playing on a sunny day.

CHAPTER TWENTY-EIGHT

Esther: Never Truly Orphaned

I N WRITING THIS book, I have strived to discover and share aspects of the greatest Jewish women that are not so well known. With regard to Esther, that was not easy. *Megillas Esther* and the story of her life is, after all, one of the most well-known stories of all.

There is, however, one aspect to Esther's story that I only discovered myself a few years ago. When I did, I was amazed and very moved.

The Gemara (*Megillah* 13a) points to the following *pasuk*:

> And it was that he [Mordechai] raised Esther, his uncle's daughter, for she had neither father nor mother. And the girl was perfectly proportioned and beautiful in appearance, and when her father and mother died, he took her to him as a daughter.
>
> (*Esther* 2:7)

The Gemara poses a question regarding this *pasuk*: If it states at the beginning of the *pasuk* that she had no father or mother, why repeat it at the end?

Rav Acha answers, *It is to teach us that her father died at the moment of her conception. Her mother died during childbirth.*

The repetition emphasizes that not only did she have no

parents—she never even *knew* her parents.

To help discover Esther's story, let me take a slight diversion. I am involved in a wonderful organization called Links, which helps girls who have lost their parents. Sadly, it quickly moved from its beginnings with a group of a few girls to thousands.

At the first-ever Links Shabbaton that I attended, the organizer asked me if I would speak to one of the girls, whom I will call Malka. Her father died suddenly of a heart attack when she was only twelve years old, and her mother had just been diagnosed with liver cancer.

I would love to tell you that I knew exactly what to say and be able to tell you how to help a girl like that. The truth is that I hadn't the slightest idea what to say. Somehow, with a lot of *siyata d'Shmaya*, I seemed to find the right words, or so I was told afterward by someone with whom she shared them.

A few years later, I landed at JFK Airport with a flu I had picked up in Eretz Yisrael and a bad case of jet lag. The moment we touched down, my phone started showing the text messages that had been accumulating since I took off from Tel Aviv. One of them was a message from Links to tell me that Malka's mother had passed away.

She lived in New Jersey, and my GPS informed me it would take around two hours to drive there. The next morning, I was feeling no better and was in fact noticeably worse. I thought of all the reasons I didn't have to go visit a young girl sitting *shivah* for a second time—and I got in my car and went anyway.

My mind once more struggled to prepare sage things to share, and once more came up blank. I walked up the driveway to the *shivah* house, hoping Heaven would repeat the rescue mission it had the first time I'd met this young woman. It didn't have to.

Malka greeted me warmly, making me very glad I had decided to come. At that moment, no one else was in the house other than her sister and an aunt. As we sat opposite each other, Malka explained the story of the last few sad days. Then, she went on to assure me that even though she couldn't understand why Hashem had made this happen to her and her sister, she was one hundred percent convinced that Hashem intended it to be ultimately for the good.

I had thought I was going there to give her *chizuk*; I had actually come to receive *chizuk* from her.

Malka had chosen to become *frum* at a very young age. Before the loss of her mother, she was scheduled to fly to Eretz Yisrael to attend a seminary in Yerushalayim. She told me she was still determined to use her plane ticket and take her place there.

As I wrote this, I stopped to make a call to see how she was doing. She is now a *kallah* who is soon marrying a very sweet young man from Boro Park.

There are two roads that open up in front of someone who has suffered tragedy and loss. The first is the easier of the two. In order to take this road, the person sees himself as having been treated cruelly by the world, other people, or Hashem, and rejects them as a consequence.

The second is the much harder path. As I wrote in one of my other books, "You either become bitter or better—and the difference between the two is *I*." This path requires a person to view the events as an opportunity to become a better person, to become closer to his Creator. It is certainly not easy. But the harder a path is, the greater the rewards it offers to those who take it and persevere to the end.

This was the path taken by Malka. It was also the one taken by Esther. What led Esther on this road?

The Midrash asks, *Why did Esther rule over 127 countries? Because she was a daughter of Sarah, who lived 127 years* (*Esther Rabbah* 58:3).

The Alshich questions this explanation. In his words: *Aren't all Jewish women daughters of Sarah? And why should Sarah's life have any connection with the countries of the Persian Empire?*

Rather, in asking this question, the Midrash is addressing a fundamental problem with the story of Esther.

There are only two possible descriptions that could accurately fit Esther: she was either a *tzaddekes*—or she was not. If we assume the former, that her merit—combined with that of her people—allowed her to rescue Klal Yisrael, there is a concern that haunts this explanation. Esther did become the queen so that she could engineer their delivery, but there is a sting in the tail: She had to become the wife of a non-Jewish king to do so. If we contrast this with what happened to

Pharaoh and Avimelech, when they tried to take Sarah as a wife, we are troubled. If Esther was a *tzaddekes*, why wasn't she similarly protected from marriage to a *rasha* like Achashveirosh?

Alternatively, if you argue that she was not a *tzaddekes*, that would certainly explain the reason that she was taken in the first place. You can assume that she made no attempt to hide her beauty and willingly joined the other women who lined up to "audition" for the part of Vashti's replacement. What other explanation could there be to explain how an inconspicuous orphan was plucked from her own house and from among her people? It could only be that she rejected the *derech* of a Jewish girl to stay at home and instead paraded her beauty in front of everyone.

Yet this suggestion is unsatisfactory, too, and presents its own puzzle. How could someone like that be the vehicle that Hashem chose with which to save the Jewish people from annihilation?

Rather, it is obvious that since everything came about through Esther, she was clearly a holy woman. That is precisely why the Midrash singles her out as the daughter of Sarah, to intimate that she was a *tzaddekes* like her ancestor. The connection of both through the number 127, too, was not coincidence—in particular, at the beginning of his reign, Achashveirosh actually ruled 240 countries but went on to lose control of 113 of them! The number that remained, 127, connects the two together and points to their equivalence to each other in *ruchniyus*.

If Sarah was miraculously spared from Pharaoh's attempt to take her from her husband, it was in order to save the Jewish people. Everything that happened to Avraham and Sarah happened to their children. *Chazal* explain that Sarah's petition to Hashem to prevent Pharaoh's evil intentions toward her allowed the Jewish women, during the exile in Egypt, to stop any Egyptian man's advances toward them. This was actually one of the three crucial factors that justified Bnei Yisrael's redemption from Egypt. It came from Sarah.

Esther being taken and forced to marry Achashveirosh was similarly done in order that the Jewish people would be saved. The way that would happen in her lifetime would necessitate no openly miraculous intervention; nevertheless, it would achieve the hoped-for result.

Pursuing the explanation as to why the Purim story had to be constructed upon hidden miracles, and not the open ones like of the Exodus, lies beyond the scope of this book. However, I will pause to offer the beginning of an explanation.

The Rambam teaches, *All the books of the* Nevi'im *and* Kesuvim *will be nullified in the days of Mashiach. The exception is the book of* Esther (*Hilchos Megillah* 2:18).

Why is such importance attributed to *Megillas Esther* that it will be the sole book that remains of *Nach* after the coming of Mashiach?

The miracles of Egypt were on a scale and openness that robbed those witnessing them their freedom of choice. Even Pharaoh's magicians told him, *This is the finger of God* (*Shemos* 8:19). Those who saw Hashem as clearly as the generation who stood at Mount Sinai had no choice but to say, *Na'aseh v'nishma*—"We will do and we will hear!" This gives future generations the argument that they are entitled to be released from the "deal." They could claim that after seeing Hashem so clearly, they had been *forced* to accept the Torah. The choice was taken from them.

Megillas Esther is the antithesis of the *parshah* of the Exodus. Purim is the antithesis of Pesach. In the Purim story, Hashem is hidden. The name Esther itself means hidden-ness, and this name and the nature of the key part she played in the story of Purim is hinted at in the *pasuk*, *And I will surely hide* (haster astir) *My face on that day* (*Devarim* 31:18). The Torah makes it clear that there were to be no open miracles in Persia.

Yet the Jewish people looked to uncover the hidden miracle they had lived through. They saw and understood that the Purim story was entirely orchestrated by Hashem and was one huge, collective, open miracle, after all. They even volunteered to accept an additional mitzvah to the 613 they previously accepted at Mount Sinai: the annual reading of the Megillah. Their adoption of an additional mitzvah validated their previous acceptance of all the other 613 mitzvos.

This is what the Gemara means when it states, *It is written, "They accepted [the Torah] and took upon themselves and upon their children and upon all those who might join them to keep these two days as they were recorded, at their appointed time, every year" (Esther 9:27). They actually accepted what they had accepted long before (Shabbos 88a).*

In the times of Esther, the Jewish people accepted upon themselves anew what they had already accepted at Mount Sinai. In so doing, they closed the "loophole" that might have allowed them to claim that they had been forced to accept the Torah.

In that case, Purim had to come about without open miracles, and Esther's role in her story that led to saving the Jewish people would need to be different from Sarah's role in her story. Still, both were designed to achieve precisely the same result.

Now, we return to the nature of Esther and the Alshich's description of that nature.

When introducing Mordechai in the Purim story, the Megillah says, *There was a man from Yehudah in Shushan, the capital (Esther 2:5)*. The word for man in the *pasuk, ish,* denotes a tzaddik, and we know that there were few in the history of Klal Yisrael as great as Mordechai.

A couple of *pesukim* later, the Megillah reports, *And it was that he raised Hadassah, that is Esther (Esther 2:7)*. This translation follows Rashi's rendering. The word *omein,* "raised," can also be translated as "crafted" (an *uman* is a craftsman). The *Yosef Lekach* explains that this conveys that Mordechai educated and taught Esther—he taught her and molded her in Torah and mitzvos. This translation fits better with the Alshich's explanation, as he goes on to say: Look carefully at the wording of the Megillah. It clearly demonstrates that Esther was a *tzaddekes* and that all the events in the story followed a script written by Hashem Himself.

The Gemara states that Esther was called Hadassah [literally, "myrtle"], because she was indeed *tzaddekes*. A *hadas,* after all, is a euphemism for a tzaddik, as it is written, *And he [Alexander the Great] stood among the* hadassim *[the righteous of Yerushalayim] (Zechariah 1:8)*.

When a person who is not innately a tzaddik stands among tzaddikim, that very proximity and association enables him or her to become a tzaddik. How much more potent, then, is the effect of a tzaddik on someone who is already a tzaddik! That beneficial effect is multiplied many times if the person is actually brought up and educated by the tzaddik. That is why the *pasuk* says that Mordechai *omein*, crafted, Hadassah. He caused her saintly nature to grow exponentially.

This name also points to another element of Esther's nature: Her saintliness neither withered nor changed. A *hadas* is an evergreen plant. Similarly, not only was Esther's *tzidkus* fresh and vibrant in the "spring" and "summer" of her life, while she was in Mordechai's home, but it was also fresh and vibrant in the "fall" and "winter" of her life, in the palace of Achashveirosh.

If you are skeptical about how an opulent life as the queen of an empire would not corrupt her, don't be! She was born an orphan who did not even know her mother or father. That fashioned a nature of humility. It made her the perfect example of *Chazal's* teaching, *If you keep the Torah through times of poverty, in the end you will keep it through times of riches, too* (*Avos* 4:9).

The Midrash quotes the *pasuk*, *We were like orphans who had no father* (*Eichah* 5:3) and states:

> Hashem said to the Jewish people, "You are crying and saying to Me that you are like orphans without a father? By your life, the savior I am going to create from among you will have neither father nor a mother!"
>
> (*Eichah Rabbah* 85:3)

He was, of course, referring to Esther, of whom the *pasuk* says that she had no father or mother. The *Eitz Yosef* explains regarding this statement of the Midrash: Hashem's response to the Jewish people indicates that they did not rely on Hashem as their Father and Guide, and saw themselves as orphaned, with no father. Their tears showed that they felt that Hashem had abandoned them. Ironically, though they perceived of themselves as orphans, Hashem arranged that the person who would emerge from among them to end their exile would be a real orphan, someone who had neither mother nor father. He elevated this person to a position of greatness, and she would save the entire Jewish nation.

Hashem's clear message is that the lack of a parent does not blight or condemn a child. Hashem supervises and takes control of that child's life. Likewise, the Jewish people are never orphaned permanently from their Father in Heaven. For this reason, He engineered the miracle that would restore the Jews to their land through someone whose life others would believe held little promise or prospect, a young girl who never even knew her mother or father.

There are two roads that open up in front of someone who has suffered tragedy and loss. They may come to see themselves, as the Jewish people did after the destruction of the Beis Hamikdash, as *"nebachs,"* orphaned and abandoned, with little hope. They could believe themselves justified in giving up and fulfilling people's worst expectations of them.

The second road is much harder. It was the one taken by Esther. But it is not as hard as it first appears if you are certain that Hashem is intricately involved in your life. That same supervision is promised over and over again in the Torah to Jews who have been orphaned or feel they have been. It is the crucial message of Esther's story.

I, my children and grandchildren, as well as you and yours (even if you do not have them yet), are (or will be) here because of a girl who knew neither her mother nor her father, but used that tragedy to become the person who could avert an infinitely greater one.

Amid the annual celebration of Purim, we often forget what one woman gave to secure Klal Yisrael's survival and make those celebrations possible. This is Esther's message. It is about what can be achieved when a person faces sadness and tragedy yet is certain that Hashem would never abandon them. Because at the end of the day, no Jew is ever truly orphaned.

CHAPTER TWENTY-NINE

Mrs. Sarah Rivkah Kohn

I N 1984, MONSEY was a very different town from the enormous center of Torah that it is today. At that time, a couple named Yisrael Efraim and Rosy Cutler lived there. They had married late in life—when Rosy was forty-two and Yisrael Efraim was forty-nine—yet they were blessed with a little girl, Sarah Rivkah. Both Yisrael Efraim and Rosy came from traditional Jewish families but had grown enormously in their love of Torah and mitzvos, helped along, of course, by their Monsey friends and neighbors.

At only two and a half years old, the little girl had no idea that her mother was setting out to meet with her doctor to get the results of tests. She would not have understood what it meant when the doctor explained that her mother had ovarian cancer and volunteered his prognosis that she had perhaps six weeks to live. It was only later that she would be able to understand and smile when she learned that her mother thanked the doctor for giving her the diagnosis but gave him a *mussar drashah* for offering an opinion he hadn't been asked to give.

"I am sorry," she told him, "but doctors neither know nor get to decide how long a person will live. That is exclusively in the hands of the Almighty."

As if to drive the point home, Mrs. Cutler went on to prove that his predictive abilities were hopelessly inaccurate, and lived another six years.

Sarah Rivkah turned from a toddler to a little girl without really being aware that her mother had a serious illness, even though she often had to stay with neighbors while her father was busy at work in Manhattan and her mother was in the hospital for treatment.

Mrs. Cutler worried that her only child might become spoiled since she had no siblings, so she came up with an ingenious plan to get her some. A *kiruv* program in Eretz Yisrael had proven extremely successful in encouraging young Israelis to become Torah and mitzvah observant. The problem was that very soon, they fell back again into their old circle of friends and family, and all the progress they had made evaporated. The organization figured out an original and ingenious solution. Young Israeli Jews who had become *ba'alei teshuvah* would be sent to the United States to stay with *frum* families for six months or so. They would be able to see the ideas they had learned about come to life, within the setting of the hosts with whom they stayed. The "bribe" to the Satan to let them come would be the opportunity to enjoy the excitement and adventure of being in America. The genius of the plan was that being away from their old lives would allow their new one to take hold and establish firm roots rather than quickly wither and die.

Mrs. Cutler volunteered to be one of the hosts, and suddenly, a family with two older parents and a little girl was transformed into a family of two parents and four boisterous and laughing girls. The new arrivals were given tasks to help Mrs. Cutler around the house. That way, they didn't feel that they weren't giving anything back. This arrangement proved particularly useful when Mrs. Cutler was going through her treatments.

Sarah Rivkah's childhood consequently became a happy and fun-filled time with Israeli "sisters" to play with and keep her company. Although she knew her mother was sometimes ill, she also knew that she went to the hospital and they made her better again.

Neither the seriousness of her mother's condition nor the doctor's devastating prognosis ever encroached on her young life. Her father went by bus every day to the large store where he was employed, called

Forty-Seventh Street Photo. Sarah Rivkah went to school and came home to her happy and carefree home.

When Sarah Rivkah was nine years old, her mother had to go back to the hospital to be "made better again." On Erev Rosh Hashanah, Sarah Rivkah went to visit and wish her mother a good Yom Tov. It was the last time she saw her. On Tzom Gedaliah, her father had to tell his little girl that this time, the hospital had not been able to make her mommy better, after all.

Sarah Rivkah cried her heart out. She recalls that she wanted to go and tell all her neighbors what had happened. She laughs when she reminisces at the reaction of her younger self and her innocence in assuming that she needed to tell the neighbors something that they probably already knew.

Since this little girl was only nine years old and therefore under the age of bas mitzvah, she was not obligated to sit *shivah*. Mr. Cutler offered her the choice of staying at home for a week or returning to school. Sarah Rivkah chose to go back to school. She returned to her classmates and teachers as the first girl in her school to be orphaned.

The teachers fretted and worried about how to treat the newly-orphaned nine-year-old girl. This was a new situation with which they had no experience. They decided that as the little girl seemed to be going on as normal and was doing as well in her lessons as she had before the tragedy, they wouldn't "rock the boat" and behaved toward her precisely the way they had before her mother's *petirah*.

Mrs. Kohn told me, "They thought that they shouldn't 'rock the boat.' They didn't understand that the boat had *already* been rocked."

The young Sarah Rivkah was very adept at appearing and even *feeling* that she was doing okay. It wouldn't be until later, when she reached her teens, that her grief started to emerge.

Meanwhile, Sarah Rivkah's father had to find a solution to being left on his own with a little girl to look after. His job meant he didn't get home until well after his daughter finished school. The best solution was for Sarah Rivkah to move in semi-permanently with one of the families with whom she had stayed when her mother had spent extended periods in the hospital.

She recalls that this solution didn't feel at all strange to her, and in any case, her father came to visit her every single night, even if the snow was falling and lay deep on the ground. He always wanted to hear how her day had gone and how she was doing. Those daily visits made Sarah Rivkah feel secure, knowing that her father was always there for her. On Shabbos, she went home, and that reinforced her certainty that her father loved her and was very much part of her life.

I was intrigued when she added, "The feeling of security and connection that my father created between us became the blueprint that I used to build my relationship with Hashem. It was how I felt about Him, and I was convinced that was how He felt about me."

That doesn't mean there weren't times when she felt anger about the situation into which Hashem had put her, but her solution was to sit down and "write to Him, to explain how she was feeling and why."

Mrs. Cutler left a very detailed *tzava'ah*, setting out what should be said at her *levayah*. She had written a list of all those who should be thanked for their help and support over the years. She had also told her husband that he had to remarry.

Seven months later, he did. When the *shidduch* was suggested, Mr. Cutler asked his daughter what she thought about the idea. The now ten-year-old girl, who was perforce mature beyond her years, had met the lady that might soon be moving into her home, and she had her answer for her father: "Go for it!" With his daughter's approval, he did.

After her father had been married for two months, and his new wife had settled in, Sarah Rivkah moved back home. Today, she admits that it was a tough adjustment, but it was one that did not show on her face.

"I was very open about telling people that my mother had died," she explained. It was that very openness that misled her teachers into thinking that she was doing fine. In fact, to use her own phrase, she was "open but emotionally closed."

When she went to visit her mother's grave on her *yahrtzeit*, it was to discharge an obligation and a duty. It was not to fulfill an emotional need.

Mrs. Kohn explained to me that her overwhelming feeling at that time was one of loneliness. She was, after all, an only child. That was the side of her she kept hidden. She did very well at school, becoming the valedictorian of her class, and she interacted well with other girls.

Of all the people from whom she hid her feelings, the one from whom she was particularly keen to hide them was her father. One day, when she was in the tenth grade, she was learning Chumash with a friend, and a question emerged.

The *pasuk* about honoring parents states, *Kabeid es avicha v'es imecha*—"Honor your father and your mother" (*Shemos* 20:12). The word "*es*" extends the scope of the *pasuk* beyond that suggested by the plain words. The Gemara says the mitzvah of honoring parents extends to a stepmother (*Kesubos* 103a).

What happens if the custom of the child's natural mother contradicts that of his father's second wife, the child's stepmother? Which custom would the mitzvah obligate you to follow?

Sarah Rivkah took her question to her teacher, who congratulated her on its insightfulness and originality and explained that she would need to consult a *rav* to find the answer.

A few days later, the teacher returned with an answer but then added, "I don't actually think that this is the question you were really asking!" The teacher admitted frankly that this situation was beyond her experience and wisdom. She suggested that Sarah Rivkah talk with another teacher, who had also lost a parent when she was a girl.

Discovering that other teacher was one of the most important moments in Sarah Rivkah's life. Thus began a magnificent relationship that allowed her to access the guidance that she had needed for so long. It allowed her to deal with her loneliness and her misleading openness.

After high school, Sarah Rivkah attended seminary in Brooklyn, which she loved. Once more, she excelled academically. During that year, she decided to fulfill her dream of becoming a teacher and was soon teaching fifth-grade girls.

After a while, a *shidduch* was suggested, and soon, she found her *zivug* and was married and living in Boro Park.

Around that time, she came across a book called *Saying Goodbye:*

A Handbook for Teens Dealing with Loss and Mourning. She had never before come across anything written specifically for *frum* girls in her situation. The book was a revelation for her.

Sarah Rivkah reached out to one of the two authors, Miriam Liebermann, and the two met. Mrs. Liebermann had a suggestion for her.

"Why not start a magazine for girls who have lost a parent just like you?"

By that time, Sarah Rivkah was already an editor for *Binah* magazine. The idea appealed to her, and so she got to work producing a magazine called *Links*. It contained sixteen articles for girls who had lost a parent. Ten of the articles were written by Sarah Rivkah herself using a variety of pen names. Her husband's graphic design skills were put to work, and soon, a magazine was born.

Sarah Rivkah and her husband became very busy contacting *rabbanim* and *askanim* who might be interested in getting the magazine to the people who would benefit most from it. It wasn't long before *Links* magazine had found its public.

The next evolution of the Kohns' initiative was the idea of inviting the girls whom the magazine had touched to come and meet them in their home. An evening of *chizuk* followed, which prompted one of the seven girls who showed up to offer a suggestion: Perhaps there should be more such events. Another girl wondered if it would be possible to perhaps get together for a Shabbaton.

In 2007, the first Links Shabbaton for girls was organized, and fifty girls attended. Rav Matisyahu Salomon arrived on Sunday to speak. He became a passionate supporter of Links. As he told the young women, he had lost his father when he was seven and understood their pain. Five years later, I was lucky enough to be invited to speak at one of the now annual Links Shabbatons.

The numbers attending were by then much larger, and I spoke twice that Friday night and then privately to some of the girls. My wife and I wished everyone a "good Shabbos" and, exhausted, went to our room to sleep. The next day, I learned that the girls were just getting started! Groups of them had stayed up until the wee small hours—and some the entire night—telling each other their stories and sharing their experiences.

I have attended six Links Shabbatons in all so far. All the *rabbanim* who are connected with the organization agree that this is the highlight of our year, the event we look forward to the most.

Links has now grown to include a boys' branch called "Shloimy's Club" and a branch for younger girls called "Little Links of Pearls." It has a branch in England, and, of course, the magazine that started it all is more popular than ever.

The pain these girls are experiencing is often enormous. Sarah Rivkah was lucky to find someone who had gone through the exact same experience as she did. Not only did that person share her experience, but she knew how to use it to help a fifteen-year-old girl whose "boat had already been rocked" and make sure it didn't sink. Now, as the founder and director of Links, she is doing the exact same thing, using her experience to help others.

Mrs. Kohn and her husband have been able to assemble a team of professionals and *rabbanim* who are able to help kids who have lost someone close. All the Links staff members lost family when they were young, and went through the same experience as the girls or the boys they help. That gives children in pain the confidence to allow them to help. It allows the staff to let the children know that they are not alone. Their own motto says it best: "We're in it together."

Crucially, Sarah Rivkah Kohn has enabled thousands of girls to do what she did when she used the care and concern of her father to build her relationship with Hashem. With that relationship in place, thousands of young Jewish girls have come to realize, like Esther before them, that no Jew is ever truly orphaned.

Afterword

HAVING ARRIVED AT the end of this book, I thought it appropriate to sum up its ultimate message. To do so, I return to the wisdom of someone I quoted in the introduction. Rav Zalman Sorotzkin, also known as the Lutzker Rav, was born in Lithuania in 1881. He learned in the yeshivos of Volozhin, Slabodka, and Telz and became the son-in-law of Rav Eliezer Gordon, the Telshe *rosh yeshivah*. He was a *rav* and a *rosh yeshivah* in his turn. Eventually, he settled in Eretz Yisrael.

Rav Zalman served as *rav* of a town in Belarus called Zhetel. This was the town where the Chafetz Chaim was born, and he used to refer to Rav Zalman as "my *rav*." Rav Zalman was the author of many *sefarim*, including the beloved *Oznayim LaTorah* that we quoted before.

In the collection of his *drashos* published as *Hade'ah V'hadibbur*, you find a *drashah* where he expands on the theme we cited in the introduction to this book. The *drashah* is called "Women Come First," and there, he addresses the issue of women's education.

He starts by quoting the *pasuk, And he [Avraham] moved to the mountain east of Beis El, and he pitched his tent, with Beis El to the west and Ai to the east and he built there an altar to Hashem (Bereishis* 12:8). The Midrash explains, *The word* ahaloh, *"his tent," can be read* ahalah, *"her tent." He pitched Sarah's tent before he pitched his own* (*Bereishis Rabbah* 39:15).

It is obvious that the tents that Avraham constructed were not ordinary tents. They were places where Torah was taught and learned. They were places where Avraham brought men and Sarah brought women under the wings of the *Shechinah*. The word *ohel*, "tent," is actually a euphemism for Torah, as in *And Yaakov was a complete man, sitting in tents* (*Bereishis* 25:27). The tents in which he sat was the *beis midrash* of the prophet Shem. It was the place where Yaakov went to learn Torah.

But Avraham's tent was also a place of prayer, where all the people of his time gathered to speak to Hashem. Why, then, did Avraham set up Sarah's tent before his own? If someone were to ask any Jew in our time, "Which part of the synagogue should we instruct the builders to complete first, the men's area or the women's area?" the question would seem rhetorical. The answer would be obvious—it should be the men's area. Men, after all, are required to pray three times every day, whereas many women don't pray daily at all and some only on the *Yamim Nora'im*. (Note, however, that the Rambam rules that prayer is a Torah requirement that is not governed by specific times; therefore, women are equally obligated in this mitzvah as men are—they are simply not required to pray in a *minyan*.) There are even some shuls that have no *ezras nashim* at all.

Imagine if we were to ask the same men a different question: "If you could build a Talmud Torah for boys or a Beis Yaakov for girls, which should be built first?" Everyone would unanimously point to the Gemara's statement, *The obligation is to teach the boys Torah, not the girls* (*Kiddushin* 29a). In previous generations, girls typically did not receive any formal education. It was only with great difficulty and in the face of fierce opposition that schools have opened that offer girls an education within the true spirit of Torah. But to *prioritize* girls' education over that of boys would be considered a perverse and bizarre notion.

But the founding father of the Jewish people, Avraham Avinu, completely disagreed. At the very beginning, when Jewish education began, he established precisely the opposite view. The first place of learning and *tefillah* he constructed was for women—Sarah's tent. Only then did he raise his own tent, his *beis midrash* for men.

The Torah emphasizes this fact to teach us that this was a carefully calculated act on Avraham's behalf in order to establish a blueprint for all future generations. It was to show that when it come to matters of *emunah*, women are greater than men.

This same message was sent directly by Hashem Yisbarach Himself, when the Jewish people appeared before Him at Mount Sinai and He offered us the Torah. *This is how you will speak to* Beis Yaakov *and tell* Bnei Yisrael (*Shemos* 19:3), He commanded Moshe. First, speak to the women, then to the men. The order of to whom Hashem chose to speak first was fundamental. It was Hashem's careful message that in matters of *emunah vada'as*, faith and Torah, women are greater than men.

The reasons for this are many, but they include the fact that women are innately more eager to keep mitzvos and that they are the ones who imbue their children with a love of Torah.

The Midrash adds that Hakadosh Baruch Hu said:

> Originally, I spoke to Adam first and then to Chavah, but that produced a catastrophe. By reversing the order now and offering the Torah to the women first, the men will remain loyal to Me. Were women to grow up without Torah and *emunah*, their husbands would have no hope, and neither would the world. Everything follows from the woman.
>
> (*Shemos Rabbah* 25)

Between these pages, we have seen countless examples of why this is so and exactly how Jewish women are so great. They were, in fact, truly the greatest of Klal Yisrael then—and they remain so now.